Building the Benedict Option

Building the Benedict Option

Architecture, Urban Planning, and Placemaking in a Post-Christian Culture

WARD DAVIS

WIPF & STOCK · Eugene, Oregon

BUILDING THE BENEDICT OPTION
Architecture, Urban Planning, and Placemaking in a Post-Christian Culture

Copyright © 2024 Ward Davis. All rights reserved. Except for brief quotations in critical publications or reviews, no part of this book may be reproduced in any manner without prior written permission from the publisher. Write: Permissions, Wipf and Stock Publishers, 199 W. 8th Ave., Suite 3, Eugene, OR 97401.

Wipf & Stock
An Imprint of Wipf and Stock Publishers
199 W. 8th Ave., Suite 3
Eugene, OR 97401

www.wipfandstock.com

PAPERBACK ISBN: 979-8-3852-1247-7
HARDCOVER ISBN: 979-8-3852-1248-4
EBOOK ISBN: 979-8-3852-1249-1

VERSION NUMBER 041024

Scripture quotations are from The ESV® Bible (The Holy Bible, English Standard Version®), © 2001 by Crossway, a publishing ministry of Good News Publishers. Used by permission. All rights reserved.

All images, unless otherwise noted, are from Pixabay and are used by permission.

Contents

Acknowledgments | vii
Introduction | ix

Chapter 1
The Importance of the Built Environment | 1

Chapter 2
The Early Irish Monastic Settlements | 17

Chapter 3
The Church Building: Encouraging an Upward Gaze | 28

Chapter 4
Housing: Rebuilding the Neighborhood | 38

Chapter 5
Amenities: Providing Social Infrastructure | 53

Chapter 6
The Coffee Shop: Third Spaces and Hospitality | 61

Chapter 7
The Coworking Space: Fostering Collaboration, Strengthening the Church | 67

Chapter 8
The Christian Education Building: Restoring the Foundation | 75

Chapter 9
The Construction: Planting the Trees Your Grandchildren Will Sit Under | 84

Chapter 10
Charting a Course Forward | 91

Chapter 11
Hurdles to Clear | 95

Chapter 12
Mission Chattanooga | 105

Chapter 13
Third Spaces and Starting a Ben Op Community from Scratch | 122

Chapter 14
The Importance of Navigators | 127

Conclusion | 132
Bibliography | 137

Acknowledgments

First off, I would like to thank my advisor, David Horn. This book is the result of my graduate work at Gordon-Conwell Theological Seminary and wouldn't have happened without his unflagging support and encouragement.

I'd also like to thank a few people who very graciously took the time to read my manuscript and provide invaluable feedback and advice: Eric Clay, Sara Joy Proppe, Amy Sherman, and, Matt Busby.

I'd like to thank Brent Campbell, who has been kind enough to mentor me in the area of real estate development and allow me to join his team and watch while he works to create an actual village using the principles of the New Urbanism.

I'd like to thank the guys from the Wednesday Group: Elijah Grubb, Santosh Ninan, Elijah Beltz, and Jordan Cooper. One of the greatest joys in my life over the past five years has been rediscovering the blessing of deep friendship through our time together. You've helped me grow intellectually and spiritually, and enriched my life greatly.

Very importantly, I'd like to thank my best friend, most faithful supporter, and the one who's done more than anyone else to help me grow into the man God wants me to be: my wife, Betty. I love you.

And finally, I'd like to thank my Lord, Jesus Christ. Soli Deo Gloria.

Introduction

I arise today,
Through the strength of heaven:
Light of sun
Brilliance of moon
Splendor of fire
Speed of lightning
Swiftness of wind
Depth of sea
Stability of earth
Firmness of rock.

—St. Patrick

In his book *The Benedict Option*, Rod Dreher issued a timely warning to the church. In an attempt to engage the broader culture with the gospel it had failed to create a distinct Christian culture and instead been coopted by American consumer culture. The result was an anemic church ill-prepared to face a quickly darkening cultural landscape and civilizational decline. In response, Dreher argued, following the example of Benedict of Nursia (the founder of European Monasticism), it was time for the church to develop new ways of "doing" church. It was time to create new institutions and strategies to help it better form disciples, minister to the broader

INTRODUCTION

culture, and survive the years ahead. It was time for a "Benedict Option."

This is my attempt to provide a template for how the leaders in a local church might go about creating their own Benedict Option community (Ben Op community). One of my frustrations with the American church is that, in our chronological snobbery, we have too quickly thrown out the hard-won experience of past generations of church leaders that I believe might offer us models for doing ministry today: far more effective models, in fact, than those we've followed for the past forty years. The early Irish monastic movement is one such model that has much to commend itself. And as Philip Bess points out, the Irish:

> *Converted Europe to Christianity . . . not by preaching alone, or perhaps even primarily; [but] by embodying Christian faith and virtue in their lives—and, not least, the physical organization of their communities.*[1]

I therefore look specifically at the early Irish monastic movement for principles church leaders today can use to develop their own Ben Op community or "modern monastic settlement." In the process, I provide the reader a brief introduction to architecture, urban planning, and place-making and explain why an understanding of these disciplines is necessary to create a healthy, effective Ben Op community.

Chapter 1: The Importance of the Built Environment

I refer to our current mental health crisis resulting from the increasing atomization of our culture, and the often overlooked role that our built environment plays in this process. I point out the very real effect the built environment has on human flourishing, point out the problem with current urban planning, and argue that the church needs to reclaim a vision for the built environment as part of the cultural mandate given to Adam and Eve.

---

1. Bess, *Till We Have Built Jerusalem*, 129.

Introduction

Chapter 2: The Early Irish Monastic Settlements

I introduce the reader to the early Irish monastic movement and the strategy it used to develop vibrant, holistic communities of faith that were able to evangelize the broader society and repair the fraying social fabric of a Western Europe descending into chaos. I suggest a new model for "doing" church patterned after the Irish way that involves the creation of Ben Op communities, "modern monastic settlements," that can both nurture a vibrant, robust Christian community while more effectively serving as cultural change agents.

Chapter 3: The Church Building—Encouraging an Upward Gaze

In this chapter I examine the importance the Irish placed on sacred architecture for encouraging a sense of awe and discuss the first and most important building of any Ben Op community: the church. I explain why non-churched people prefer traditional sacred architecture over "big bland boxes" and in the process make the case for why we should prefer traditional architecture over modern.

Chapter 4: Housing—Rebuilding the Neighborhood

In contrast with later monastic communities that consisted primarily of clergy, Irish monastic settlements often were composed of clergy, laity, and families all living together. This ensured that an important part of such settlements was variety of housing. In this chapter, I therefore argue that every Ben Op community should involve some form of housing, both as a means of strengthening the life of the Ben Op community itself as well as repairing the social fabric of the broader community. I introduce the reader to the concept of "missing middle" housing and discuss the important role shared space can have in nurturing a sense of community and offering positive health benefits.

Introduction

Chapter 5: Amenities—Providing Social Infrastructure

The faith practiced by many evangelical Christians is often an intensely personal faith with little impact on life outside of Sundays. In contrast, the Irish practiced a faith that spoke to all life. This was reflected in the myriad types of buildings they included in their monastic settlements: the "social infrastructure" they incorporated into their communities. In this chapter I explore the idea of social infrastructure, why it contributed to the success of Irish settlements, and how modern Ben Op communities can use it to nourish "thick" community and contribute to the overall health of their city, town, or suburb.

Chapter 6: The Coffee Shop—Third Spaces and Hospitality

One of the Irish monks' highest commitments was hospitality to strangers, seekers, pilgrims, and refugees. In an insecure and often violent world the monastic communities they built were intended to be havens of security. By practicing hospitality and creating havens of peace, monasteries began to affect the culture of the broader society. In this chapter, I suggest ways a Ben Op community can begin to affect its surrounding community, by providing hospitality through "third spaces"—places like coffee shops that aren't home or work, but that treat the clientele as members of the community.

Chapter 7: The Coworking Space—Fostering Collaboration, Strengthening the Church

The Irish monks who set about re-evangelizing and re-civilizing Western Europe knew that they were a minority group, surrounded by a largely hostile, or at best, indifferent culture. Their approach of creating monastic settlements recognized that in order to successfully penetrate and transform their culture, they first had to create a structure that would nourish, support, and protect a distinctly alternative/Christian culture. I suggest one way a Ben Op

Introduction

community could do this is by the creation of coworking sites for Christian organizations. Potential benefits of such sites include: increased collaboration between the body of Christ, intellectual ferment provided by a gathering of leaders, and, potentially, networks of such leaders working together to effect broad cultural change.

Chapter 8: The Christian Education Building—Restoring the Foundation

Monastic settlements created by the Irish were centers of education that preserved the cultural heritage of the West as the Roman Empire gradually disintegrated. We face a similar situation today. Increasingly, younger generations are losing the civic and historical knowledge required to sustain our culture. In addition, by handing over the education of our youth to a hostile educational establishment the church has ensured that each successive generation is more secular and hardened to spiritual truth than the last. Ben Op communities will make the recovery of Christian classical education central to their mission. By doing so, they will help the church reclaim its role as the primary educator and disciple maker of its youth while, at the same time, blessing the broader community by making an excellent education available to all.

Chapter 9: The Construction—Planting the Trees Your Grandchildren Will Sit Under

Although the Irish monks built well over a thousand years ago, some of the buildings they built still exist today. That any of the modern homes (and other buildings) we've constructed over the past fifty years will still exist in a thousand years is almost inconceivable. A focus on short-term profit on the part of the housing industry and a rootless, atomized culture have led to a situation where, today, the quality and durability of the houses we build are far below what was built even a hundred years ago. In fact, we're losing the very skills to build lasting, quality buildings. In contrast,

Introduction

when we build our Ben Op communities, we need to possess a long-term vision and focus on constructing buildings of quality and durability that will last for centuries.

Chapter 10: Charting a Course Forward

When bands of Irish monks set out across Europe to plant the monastic settlements that would later grow to become towns and cities, it was a harder but much simpler time. Today, creating a Ben Op community requires navigating a byzantine process and complying with countless ordinances. In this chapter, I lay out the basic real estate development process you'll have to go through to take your vision for a Ben Op community and make it a reality.

Chapter 11: Hurdles to Clear

From restrictive zoning regulations, to financing, to community opposition, in this chapter I look at a number of potential hurdles you may need to clear while seeking to build your Ben Op community. I also address the question, "What if we already have an existing building?" by suggesting various ways a faith community can look to repurpose an already existing building.

Chapter 12: Mission Chattanooga

I examine a modern day monastic settlement of intrepid trailblazers, who through the principles laid out in this book are using the built environment in innovative ways to strengthen the church and impact their community in profound ways. The folks at Mission Chattanooga freely offer hard won lessons to anyone seeking to create their own modern monastic settlement and create a truly impactful Ben Op community.

Introduction

Chapter 13: Third Spaces and Starting a Ben Op Community from Scratch

What should you do if you're seeking to build a Ben Op community from scratch? While it might be tempting to utilize traditional church planting techniques, in this chapter, I suggest instead the possibility of using a third space.

Chapter 14: The Importance of Navigators

Leading a faith community is extremely difficult on multiple levels. It requires a leader to be conversant in a number of disciplines. Expecting them also to be conversant in real estate development and architecture seems a bit much. This is why in the development of your Ben Op community, it will be important to find trustworthy, knowledgeable guides, who can help you navigate the often treacherous shoals presented by urban planning and real estate development. This chapter introduces the reader to individuals and organization that can help to educate them as they seek to develop the skills necessary to build their own Ben Op community.

Conclusion

By contrasting the vision of hell given by C. S. Lewis in his work *The Great Divorce* with the picture of the new Jerusalem found in the book of Revelation, I make a final case for why the built environment should be a crucial part of the church's cultural mission and thus something to be considered carefully in the development of any Benedict Option community.

By focusing on the built environment, by no means do I mean to imply that architecture and urban planning are preeminent concerns for the church—merely that they are often neglected or overlooked by church leaders when thinking about church planting or new construction. There already exist several books suggesting ways to develop a Ben Op community that focus on the spiritual practices/framework required to do so—but none that I'm aware of that focus on the actual construction and layout of such communities and why this is important. And it is just in this area of construction and real estate that church leaders, particularly pastors, are often most unfamiliar.

There are myriad books on church leadership and church planting. There are not that many on urban planning and architecture and what they mean for the way we conceive of "doing church."

As mentioned earlier, one of my frustrations with the American church is that, in our chronological snobbery, we have too quickly thrown out the hard-won experience of past generations of church leaders who I believe offer more effective models for "doing" church. The early Irish monastic movement is one such model that has much to commend itself. It is my hope that this work will encourage readers to consider it as a model worth emulating, particularly as we look for innovative ways to build Ben Op communities that will not only help the church to weather the years ahead, but begin to turn the cultural tide.

Chapter 1

The Importance of the Built Environment

For the role of religion in human life is not little. It is essential: without it there is no culture at all, because culture is a cultivation of the things that a people considers most sacred.

—ANTHONY ESOLEN, *OUT OF THE ASHES*

What's Going On?

America is currently in the grip of an epidemic of anxiety and other mental disorders. Anxiety disorders—including generalized anxiety disorder, panic disorder, and social anxiety, among others—are the most common mental illness in the US, affecting some forty million adults every year.[1] In 1980, only 4 percent of Americans suffered from an anxiety disorder. Today, an estimated 19.1 percent of US adults struggle with some form of anxiety.[2] From 1999 to 2016, according to the CDC, almost every state but one saw an increase in

---

1. Honderich, "Panel Says U.S. Adults Should Get."
2. Harvard Medical School, "National Comorbidity Survey," Data Table 2: 12-month prevalence DSM-IV/WMH-CIDI disorders by sex and cohort.

the rate of suicide,[3] and a 2001 paper published by the Bureau of Economic Analysis found that the suicide rate tripled between 1950 and 1990.[4]

Adolescents seem particularly hard hit. Research throughout the last several decades has shown a consistent pattern of rising anxiety, depression, suicide, and suicide attempts among American adolescents. According to a study published in *Translational Psychiatry*, 36 percent of teenage girls are depressed or have suffered a recent major depressive episode. The pandemic has obviously had a tremendous impact on the mental health of adolescents, but even before the advent of the virus, researchers were sounding the alarm. Jean Twenge, writing in 2017, argued that adolescents were on the brink of the worst mental health crisis in decades.[5] Past generations of Americans who lived through the Great Depression and experienced the trauma of World War II reported far lower levels of anxiety and depression.[6] What's causing this epidemic of anxiety depression, loneliness, and suicide? What's going on?

3. Centers for Disease Control and Prevention, "Suicide Rising."
4. Charen, "Kids Are Not All Right," §2.
5. Twenge, "Have Smart Phones Destroyed a Generation?"
6. Charen, "Kids Are Not All Right," §3.

One Possible Clue

One clue may be found, surprisingly enough, in the opioid epidemic currently ravaging many communities. Commenting on the popularity of opioids, Andrew Sullivan writes:

> It is significant, it seems to me, that the drugs now conquering America are downers: They are not the means to engage in life more vividly but to seek a respite from its ordeals. The alkaloids that opioids contain have a large effect on the human brain because they tap into our natural "mu-opioid" receptors. The oxytocin we experience from love or friendship is chemically replicated by the molecules derived from the poppy plant. It's a shortcut—and an instant intensification—of the happiness we might ordinarily experience in a good and fruitful communal life.[7]

Sullivan is not the only person to highlight this connection. As Eric Klinenberg points out, "Intriguingly, there's a growing body of neurological research showing that opioids are, [in fact] chemically speaking, a good analog for social connection."[8] So, if Sullivan and Klinenberg are correct, one reason so many Americans are experiencing rising anxiety, depression, and loneliness may be due in part to a lack of meaningful community.

Roseto, Pennsylvania

The impact community has on the wellbeing of individuals went largely unrecognized until a doctor named Stewart Wolf noticed something quite surprising about a small town nestled among the hills of rural Pennsylvania named Roseto. Sometime in the late fifties, at a local medical society gathering the town doctor met Dr. Stewart Wolf, head of medicine of the University of Oklahoma. Over coffee afterwards, the local doctor related to Wolf how he rarely saw anyone from Roseto under the age of sixty-five with heart disease.

---

7. Sullivan, "Poison We Pick," §4–5.
8. Klinenberg, *Palaces for the People*, 119.

> *Wolf was taken aback. This was the 1950's, years before the advent of cholesterol lowering drugs and aggressive measures to prevent heart disease. Heart attacks were an epidemic in the United States. They were the leading cause of death in the men under the age of sixty-five. It was impossible to be a doctor, common sense said, and not see heart disease.*[9]

Intrigued, Wolf decided to investigate and gathered a team of researchers from Oklahoma University.

Beginning in 1961, with the full support of the entire town, Wolf's team began an exhaustive study of the residents of Roseto. The results were shocking—virtually no one under sixty-five showed any signs of heart disease or had died of a heart attack. As their research continued, their results became even more surprising. They found that there was no drug addiction, no alcoholism, no suicides, and very little crime. People were literally dying of old age. The researchers' first thoughts were that the unusual quality of life and health enjoyed by residents was a result of their diet and exercise. This proved a dead end. Then they examined whether the residents' genetic makeup was responsible, and finally they investigated whether there was something about Roseto's location that was affecting longevity. No luck. Finally, after extensive investigation, Wolf came to the surprising conclusion that the unusual health and well-being of the residents of Roseto were owing to the depth and strength of the community they enjoyed. "'The community,' Wolf says, 'was very cohesive. There was no keeping up with the Joneses. Houses were very close together, and everyone lived more or less alike.'" Elders were revered and incorporated into community life. Housewives were respected, and fathers ran the families.[10]

Or, as Malcolm Gladwell puts it in his book *Outliers*, the residents of Roseto enjoyed exceptional mental and physical health because they "had created a powerful, protective social structure

---

9. Gladwell, *Outliers*, 6.
10. Bowden and Sinatra, *Great Cholesterol Myth*, 240.

capable of insulating them from the pressures of the modern world."[11]

Social Capital

This ability of community to positively affect the health and well-being of individuals has come to be known as the "Roseto Effect," and it is one reason sociologists like Harvard's Robert Putnam have been so alarmed by the breakdown in the United States over the past fifty years of what they call social capital. Putnam defines social capital as the "features of social organization such as networks, norms, and social trust that facilitate coordination and cooperation for mutual benefit."[12] As he puts it:

> For a variety of reasons, life is easier in a community blessed with a substantial stock of social capital. In the first place, networks of civic engagement foster sturdy norms of generalized reciprocity and encourage the emergence of social trust. Such networks facilitate coordination and communication, amplify reputations, and thus allow dilemmas of collective action to be resolved.[13]

Putnam, in his book *Bowling Alone*, examines a myriad of indicators showing the increasing breakdown of social capital in the United States over the past fifty years. From fewer people voting, to fewer parents involved in the PTA, to a decline in union membership, to less involvement in the Boy Scouts, Red Cross, and fraternal organizations, Americans' civic engagement and community involvement have plummeted over the past fifty years.[14]

But what is to account for this fraying of the communal fabric with the resulting loss of social capital? Various answers have been given. Putnam points, however reluctantly, to the increasing diversity of our society as one factor. Others point to the decline

11. Gladwell, *Outliers*, 9.
12. Putnam, "Bowling Alone," 2.
13. Putnam, "Bowling Alone," 2.
14. Putnam, "Bowling Alone," 4.

in stable, long-term marriages and the increase in more people opting not to have children—leaving people without an extended family to help them face their later years. Zygmunt Bauman points to liquid modernity, the characteristics of modern life: "fragility, temporariness, vulnerability and inclination to constant change."[15] Other scholars such as Patrick Deneen point to the very nature of liberalism itself, which dissolves the ties that bind until increasingly we are left as rootless consumers. All of these commentators, however, overlook one of the chief problems contributing to the fraying of our social fabric: our built environment. The way we plan our communities and design our buildings not only serves to reduce social capital but also negatively affects us in a myriad of unintended ways. And nothing is more responsible for this situation than the automobile.

The Problem with Urban Planning

After World War II, the United States set its face toward the future with a renewed sense of confidence. As the only major Western economy to survive the war not only untouched but supercharged, it promoted an American dream fueled by consumer goods and epitomized by the house in the suburbs and, above all, the automobile. The construction of the interstate highway system encouraged a life centered on mobility and contributed to a trend in urban planning to build communities to fit not the human being, but the automobile.

As Victor Papanek puts it:

> *Modern planners are so concerned about traffic that they have stopped thinking about anything but the fastest movement of cars and the attendant problems, as if the only function of the city is to serve as a racetrack for drivers between petrol pumps and hamburger stands.*[16]

---

15. Bauman, *Liquid Modernity*, viii.
16. Anonymous, "Victor Papanek Post."

The Importance of the Built Environment

Eric Klinenberg in his book *Palaces for the People* points out that "when people engage in sustained, recurrent interaction, particularly while doing things they enjoy, relationships inevitably grow."[17] The problem is that designing our communities to be "car-centric" has led to a zoning system that reinforces the fragmentation of life, where the different constituent parts of life are isolated from one another. We live in one geographic area, work in another, shop in another, worship in another, and recreate in another. The result is that we interact with one another less and consequently have fewer relationships: our social capital is decreased. The neighborhoods we've created, rather than being genuine communities, are, in the words of Ross Chapin, "merely collections of individual houses, each an island in itself, with little real connection among neighbors."[18]

Another way that the design of our communities reduces social capital is by grouping people according to socioeconomic status. Sociologists point out that whereas once there was a common American culture that served to unite people across the socioeconomic spectrum, increasingly, people are grouping according to

17. Klinenberg, *Palaces for the People*, 5.
18. Chapin, *Pocket Neighborhoods*, 7.

income. Our suburbs have only served to reinforce this trend. As Chuck Marohn points out:

> Zoning, as well as land covenants and property associations, create uniformity across each new neighborhood that is built. Not only are all homes on a given cul-de-sac built within a few years of each other, they are all built in a tight price range. Homes are clustered together by price, with a buffer between them and homes in a different price point. Homes for the modestly wealthy family are in a completely different pod from homes for the very wealthy, even though they are both wealthy by American standards. Those pods are disconnected from each other and separated by buffers, as if someone driving a Lexus would be injured by living in proximity to someone merely driving a Buick. This kind of stratification happens for all classes of society. Modern city-building efficiently creates pods of static, monocultural development.[19]

So not only do our communities keep our life fragmented, they further reduce social capital by separating us according to socioeconomic status.

In addition to lowering social capital, the way we design our communities also places an undue financial burden on families and individuals by making it almost impossible to get by without a car. To utilize our public transportation system, in all but the largest metropolitan areas, is an exercise in patience, long-suffering, and in some cases, futility. By designing our communities around the automobile, we require people at the very bottom of the socioeconomic ladder to put an inordinate amount of their money toward the purchase and maintenance of an automobile just to survive. According to some studies, the annual cost of owning a car can range from between ten thousand dollars to twelve thousand dollars.[20] If we designed our communities differently, low-wage earners could put this money aside for education, housing,

---

19. Marohn, *Strong Towns*, 21–22.
20. Delbridge, "What Is the True Cost," §9.

or other needs, thus reducing financial hardship and increasing their likelihood of long-term financial security.

Our car-centric development also may contribute to an unhealthy lifestyle by reducing the time Americans spend walking. According to the CDC, obesity-related conditions such as stroke, heart disease, type 2 diabetes, and certain types of cancer are among the leading causes of preventable premature death,[21] and there has been an increase in the obesity rate of 11 percentage points between 2000 and 2020.[22] Americans have one of the highest rates of obesity among developed nations,[23] and whereas in other developed countries obesity is responsible for only 2 to 4 percent of national health expenditures, in the United States obesity is responsible for 6 to 10 percent of national health expenditures.[24] One reason for the increase in obesity among Americans may be because we walk far less than other nationalities. A 2017 study to discover which countries were most active and which were the least found that the United States ranked thirtieth among the forty-six countries studied.[25]

Not only does the design of our communities encourage an unhealthy lifestyle, it also degrades the environment. The average suburban neighborhood is zoned for single-family houses and typically mandates that houses are separated from other houses by large lots and include large setbacks from the road. This means lower density and it increases the distance that people have to travel to get anywhere. In most cases this increases reliance on the automobile and means increased pollution and decreased habitat for wildlife.

And finally, another problem with the way we design our communities is that they are financially unsustainable. Charles Marohn and the Strong Towns movement have shown convincingly that

---

21. Centers for Disease Control and Prevention, "Overweight and Obesity," §1.
22. Centers for Disease Control and Prevention, "Overweight and Obesity."
23. Bartrina, "Prevalence of Obesity in Developed Countries."
24. Bleich et al., "Why Is the Developed World Obese?"
25. Gunaratna, "Daily Step Counts," §4.

the development model currently followed by most municipalities in America, that prioritizes low-density, single family, suburban sprawl and relies on vast infusions of federal money upfront, fails to generate enough of a tax base for long-term fiscal sustainability.[26] James Kunstler makes a similar case, arguing that our current method of development is unsustainable and that we are headed inevitably toward a breakdown of the complicated mechanisms that support modern life, or what he calls "the long emergency." As Marohn puts it:

> *Our cities are going to contract geographically; we will have fewer lane miles, fewer pipes, and less urbanized land in three decades than we do today. This is built into the math. . . . We're not going to keep and maintain every cul-de-sac, interchange or frontage road that has been built. It's not [financially] possible. . . . In a very real sense, many of our infrastructure systems are going to completely fail, while neighborhoods will be abandoned, and cities will shrink geographically.*[27]

The New Urbanists

Beginning in the late eighties and early nineties, there's been an increasing realization on the part of planners, urban designers, architects, and engineers that something was wrong. This feeling eventually strengthened and coalesced into a movement called New Urbanism.

> *New Urbanism is a planning and development approach based on the principles of how cities and towns had been built for the last several centuries: walkable blocks and streets, housing and shopping in close proximity, and accessible public spaces. In other words: New Urbanism focuses on human-scaled urban design.*[28]

---

26. Marohn, *Strong Towns*; see especially chapter 3.
27. Marohn, *Strong Towns*, 108–9.
28. Congress for the New Urbanism, "What Is New Urbanism?," §1.

The Problem with the Church

Despite this growing realization on the part of the New Urbanists of the way the built environment contributes to health and wellbeing, by and large, the church has remained blind to this fact. In fact, if anything, the church has often merely contributed to the problem. Why? According to Charles Taylor, because it has been caught up in a cultural process of what he calls "excarnation" that involves "the steady disembodying of spiritual life, so that it is less and less carried in deeply meaningful bodily forms, and lies more and more in the head."[29] Or as James K. A. Smith puts it, it has become a church characterized by "disembodiment and abstraction, an aversion of and flight from the particularities of embodiment (and communion)."[30]

Encouraging this shift has been a focus in some Christian circles that tends to see humans as primarily thinking beings. Because we are thinking beings, therefore, the intellect is paramount. And so, the focus of corporate worship is the sermon, and discipleship is seen as primarily a matter of changing the way one thinks. As James K. A. Smith puts it:

> *In ways that are more "modern" than biblical, we have been taught to assume that human beings are fundamentally thinking beings. . . . Like Descartes, we view our bodies as (at best!) extraneous, temporary vehicles for trucking around our souls or "minds," which are where all the real action takes place. . . . [Such thinking] reduces humans to brains-on-a-stick.*[31]

Another current within Evangelicalism that has contributed to a lack of appreciation for our built environment is that of a theology gripped by a sense of Jesus' imminent return. Time is short, and therefore, there is a focus on saving as many people as possible, as quickly as possible (to the exclusion of all else). Such a theology sees an appreciation for our built environment as little

---

29. Taylor, *Secular Age*, 771.
30. Smith, *How (Not) To Be Secular*, 58.
31. Smith, *You Are What You Love*, 3.

more than rearranging deck chairs on the Titanic. While we might agree with C. S. Lewis that "the salvation of a single soul is more important than the production or preservation of all the epics and tragedies in the world,"[32] the danger inherent in such an approach is that if Christ does delay, we put off the much-needed work of transforming culture (and with it the built environment), while the church continues to lose ground.

While the currents just mentioned flow from within the church, a fourth current, this time rippling out from the broader culture, has also contributed to the church's lack of appreciation for the built environment: the rise and triumph of an autonomous "self," unmoored from any grounding in physicality or created order.

One hundred years ago, if a man came to a doctor and told him he was a woman trapped in a man's body, the doctor would attempt to bring the man's thinking in line with his body. Today, if a man complained of the same thing to a doctor, the doctor is apt to attempt to shape the man's body to bring it into line with his thinking.[33] This is nothing less than the resurrection of the old gnostic heresy that sees matter as something secondary to the true, more important "self." Identity is something to be constructed *ex nihilo*, rather than, as past generations saw it, something to be determined by our physical body and our embeddedness in a physical community.

This emphasis on the autonomous self, coinciding with a gradual belittling of the created world, can be seen most clearly in the rise of Mark Zuckerberg's Metaverse and the rise of a transhumanism that seeks to overcome death by uploading one's consciousness to the web. One reason for the church's lack of appreciation for the built environment, I contend, is because it has been influenced more than it realizes by this trend toward Gnosticism in the broader society.

---

32. Lewis, *Mind Awake*, 128.

33. This point was made by Carl Trueman at an event hosted by the Chesterton House, a Christian study center at Cornell University.

The Importance of the Built Environment

The influence of these currents of thought have ensured that evangelical Christianity has little appreciation for the physical world and little interest in changing culture. What seems to be lacking is a robust sacramental theology. This has led to buildings with an impoverished architecture, no sense of aesthetics or beauty, and no reflection of literally thousands of years of history, culture, and sacred architectural language. It has been said that cathedrals are Bibles in stone, that our very churches speak. Today, our churches are mute, and if they do speak, they speak the language of a world in which the autonomous self is increasingly seen as the center of all things, defining its own reality, and where life is ordered primarily for the comfort of the individual. Our churches don't speak of the glory of God, or draw our thoughts higher, or make us aware of our position vis-à-vis a holy God.

Marginalization

In addition, the very location of our churches speaks to the church's blindness to the importance of the built environment. As Philip Bess points out:

> The pre-1945 American city was the embodiment of legitimate authority, characterized by the architectural hierarchy wherein the most prominent buildings sheltered communal buildings—those institutions necessary for the promotion of those moral, theological and intellectual virtues essential for both individual and communal well-being. It was fitting that such buildings . . . be both durable and visible.[34]

Historically, the mainline denominations understood this. They recognized the importance of real estate and the important role played in the civic life of community, and understood the truth expressed by Abraham Kuyper, that "there is not a square inch in the whole domain of our human existence over which Christ, who

---

34. Bess, *Till We Have Built Jerusalem*, 218.

Building the Benedict Option

is Sovereign over all, does not cry, Mine!"[35] Therefore, churches were built at the very center of cities and towns, reflecting God's rule over all life. Churches had a seat at the table and a voice in the important conversations of the day.

Over the past fifty years, however, the rather cultured but anemic mainline denominations have withered and been pushed aside by a brash evangelical church. In contrast with most mainline churches, the majority of evangelical churches have been built in isolation, in suburbs far from the center, and do nothing to ameliorate the fragmentation of modern America. In fact, because of the way we have designed our communities over the past seventy years, increasingly, there are no longer any city centers: merely an undifferentiated suburban sprawl that increases our sense of anomie and isolation.

Instead of attempting to counter this drift, evangelical churches have only served to worsen the problem and further reinforce the idea that faith is something private, something isolated from the rest of life. Nothing better represents the increasing marginalization of Christianity itself in American life. With the exception of the realm of politics, the church has not so much

---

35. Abraham Kuyper, "Sphere Sovereignty," cited in Henderson, "Kuyper's Inch."

The Importance of the Built Environment

been pushed out of the public square as it has abandoned it. The arts, education, city planning, civic engagement, environmental conservation, historic preservation, and myriad other disciplines related to the public square have all but been abandoned by the church. Why? Because they've been seen as irrelevant to its true mission of saving souls. But as Robert Louis Wilken remind us:

> *Christ entered history as a community, a society, not simply as a message, and the form taken by the community's life is Christ within society. The church is a culture in its own right. Christ does not simply infiltrate a culture; Christ creates culture by forming another city, another sovereignty with its own social and political life.*[36]

And an integral part of any culture is its built environment: its architecture, the design of its cities, its neighborhoods. Therefore, the church needs to regain a sacramental theology that is not only concerned with saving people's souls, but also with culture making. Specifically, it needs to look for ways to use the built environment to help support its task of redeeming culture and blessing the community in which it is embedded, while serving as a base for proclaiming the gospel. To do so is to reclaim our *imago Dei*, that, in the words of James K. A. Smith, "is not a thing or property that was lost; [but] a calling and a vocation that Adam and Eve failed to carry out . . . Adam and Eve were called to be God's vice-regents, God's cultural agents mediating His love and care for creation."[37] This means that our vocation as humans remains to complete the creational task given to Adam, and this includes our built environment. Or, as Smith puts it, "We fulfill the mission of being God's image bearers by undertaking the work of culture making."[38]

As mentioned in my introduction, in his book *The Benedict Option*, Rod Dreher issued a timely warning to the church. In an attempt to engage the broader culture it had failed to create its own distinct Christian culture and instead been coopted by the broader

---

36. Wilken, "Church as Culture," §8.
37. Smith, *Desiring the Kingdom*, 164–65.
38. Smith, *Desiring the Kingdom*, 165.

culture. The result has been an evangelical church ill-prepared to face a quickly darkening cultural landscape. In response, Dreher argued, following the example of Benedict of Nursia, it was time for the church to develop new ways of "doing" church. It was time to create new institutions and strategies to help it better develop its own distinctive and robust Christian culture, form disciples, minister to the broader culture, and survive the years ahead. It was time for a "Benedict Option."

In this book, I propose to look for historical models that might inform our approach to the built environment and, guided by the principles of New Urbanism, develop a template to guide future church construction that would help counteract suburban sprawl, help mend our fraying social fabric, and create our own Ben Op communities in the vast suburban wasteland in which so many of us live. In short, I want to provide a guidebook for how to build a Benedict Option community. And the historic model that I believe offers the most potential in doing so is the Irish monastic movement of late antiquity.

Chapter 2

The Early Irish Monastic Settlements

It has long seemed abundantly clear to me that I was born into a dying, if not already dead, civilization, whose literature was part of the general decomposition; a heap of rubble scavenged by scrawny Eng. Lit. vultures, and echoing with the hyena cries of Freudians looking for their Marx and Marxists looking for their Freud. This, despite Adam's apples quivering over winged collars to extol it, and money, money, money, printed off and stuffed into briefcases to finance it. At the beginning of a civilization, the role of the artist is priestly; at the end, harlequinade. From St. Augustine to St. Ezra Pound, from Plainsong to the Rolling Stones, from El Greco to Picasso, from Chartres to the Empire State Building, from Benvenuto Cellini to Henry Miller, from Pascal's Pensées *to Robinson's* Honest to God. *A Gadarene descent down which we all must slide, finishing up in the same slough.*

—Malcolm Muggeridge,
Chronicles of Wasted Time

Monasteries: Engagement, not Retreat

When the average person thinks of a monastery, they tend to think of groups of priests or nuns living in relative seclusion and dedicating their time to prayer and contemplation with little interaction or impact on their surrounding community. Put bluntly, the current, widespread view of monasteries is that they are a retreat from the world with an accompanying focus on primarily "spiritual" work. So when one raises the possibility of creating monastic communities for the twenty-first century, they are apt to be met with opposition by those who see such a suggestion as a retreat from the world into a pietistic, inward-looking world at the very time when, as never before, the church needs to be actively engaged in addressing the needs of a society in free-fall. But such a view is based on what monasteries eventually became, not what they were initially: one of the most effective strategies for penetrating and transforming culture, as well as for advancing the gospel. No monastic movement in history was more evangelistic and outward focused than that of the Irish.

As George Hunter III points out, "The Eastern monasteries were organized to protest, and escape from the materialism of the Roman world and the corruption of the church," while the Irish monasteries in contrast were "organized to penetrate the pagan world and to extend the church."[1] And as Richard Fletcher points out, "They were rightly perceived as agents for the diffusion of Christianity in society,"[2] becoming, in John Finney's words, "the evangelistic spearhead of the Irish church."[3] Therefore, rather than build their monastic communities in an inaccessible seclusion, "the Celtic Christians typically built their monasteries in locations accessible to the traffic of the time, such as proximity to settlements, on hilltops, or on islands near established sea-lanes."[4]

And while Irish monastic communities were often founded by monks and nuns, far from comprising only clergy, they were populated largely by laity. As Hunter points out:

> Priests, teachers, scholars, craftsmen, artists, cooks, farmers, families and children, as well as monks and/or nuns —all under the leadership of a lay abbot or abbess—populated the communities. They had little use for more than a handful of ordained priests, or for people seeking ordination; they were essentially lay-movements. A few, such as Bangor and Clonfert, may [even] have been as large as three thousand people.[5]

The Dissolution of the West

When Gregory the Great ascended to the seat of the papacy in AD 590, he gazed out upon a Roman Empire that was but a pale shadow of the triumphant empire that had confidently stood astride the world of antiquity. In his despair he cried out:

> I ask, what is there now in this world to please us? Everywhere we see sights of mourning and hear the groans of men. Cities are ruined, towns are desolate, fields lie waste; the land hath become a wilderness. No husbandman is left

---

1. Hunter, *Celtic Way of Evangelism*, 16.
2. Fletcher, *Barbarian Conversion*, 91.
3. Finney, *Recovering the Past*, 56.
4. Hunter, *Celtic Way of Evangelism*, 16.
5. Hunter, *Celtic Way of Evangelism*, 16.

in the fields; scarce a citizen remains in the cities; and even these scant remnants of humanity live under daily and unceasing plagues—plagues of divine justice which have no end, because the guilty actions themselves are not yet amended thereby. Some we see led into captivity, others maimed, others slain; what therefore, my brethren, do we see of pleasure in this life ? Nay, if we yet love such a world as this, it is not joys but wounds that we love.[6]

His plaintive cry expressed a forlorn longing for a Greco-Roman world of stability, law, and civilization that had been irrevocably lost. But even as he stared in despair at the wreckage of the classical world, a nascent Irish monastic movement was beginning to send out monks, known as *peregrinatti*, who would serve to not only re-evangelize an increasingly barbarian Western Europe, but also re-civilize it. And as Philip Bess reminds us, central to their strategy was the built environment:

> We mustn't forget that . . . monks . . . converted Europe to Christianity . . . not by preaching alone, or perhaps even primarily; [but] by embodying Christian faith and virtue in their lives—and, not least, the physical organization of their communities.[7]

Repairing the Social Fabric

And so, in the fading twilight of the Roman Empire in the West, evangelistic groups of Irish monks spread out over Europe with the goal of founding monasteries. Through the monasteries they founded, they helped evangelize the Germanic tribes flooding into Western Europe and helped repair the social fabric of a Roman Empire that was sliding into barbarism as "municipal and

---

6. Gregory the Great, *Homilies on the Book of the Prophet Ezekiel*, cited in Coulton, *Social Life in Britain*, 187.

7. Bess, *Till We Have Built Jerusalem*, 129.

provincial governments disintegrated and imperial appointees abandoned their posts."[8]

Before these monastic settlements showed their potential for rebuilding social infrastructure in Western Europe, they first showed their ability for building it in a rural Irish culture in which, "the settlement pattern . . . was entirely dispersed and rural and largely dependent upon a farming economy."[9] They did so by creating small islands of community, trade, economic activity, and learning, that would eventually grow into towns and in some cases cities, and so laid the foundation for broader societal development. Such "Monastic Towns"[10] thus, played an important role in the eventual urbanization of Ireland and, eventually, Western Europe. As John Blair points out:

> *The "monastic town" can be defined in two ways: as the physical expression of a late seventh-century sacred ideal realized in topography, architecture, and art; [and] as an economic centre which changed through time with the changing world around it. It is an observable fact that, as the centuries passed, the one tended to become more and more like the other, with the eventual result that a high proportion of [monastic settlements] are now urban, at least in the broad sense of being locally important market towns. Not only did [monastic settlements] look more like towns than any other kind of pre-Viking settlement; they also showed a strong tendency to become real towns as the economy developed between the ninth and twelfth centuries.*[11]

And as M. Valante indicates, such monastic settlements would eventually engage in specialized manufacturing, resulting in surrounding suburban zones. These zones would then eventually become urban and develop permanent fairs and marketplaces.[12]

8. Cahill, *How the Irish Saved Civilization*, 61.

9. Edwards, *New History of Ireland*, 238.

10. Charles Doherty first popularized this idea in 1985 in his article "Monastic Town in Early Medieval Ireland."

11. Blair, *Church in Anglo-Saxon Society*, 262.

12. Blair, *Church in Anglo-Saxon Society*, 17–18.

By the seventh century, there were hundreds of such settlements throughout Ireland. The Irish then set themselves the same goal of founding such settlements throughout a Western Europe that was reverting to a pre-civilized condition.

One of the greatest founders of such monastic communities was Columbanus. Born in Ireland in AD 540, by the time of his death in AD 640, he had founded sixty monastic communities throughout France, Germany, Switzerland, and Italy. The monastic settlements that Columbanus and other monks like him founded served not only as bases from which they preached the gospel to their surrounding culture but also helped to repair the fraying social fabric and rebuild the community of a culture being torn apart by centrifugal forces. And, ultimately, these monastic communities became the nuclei of what would become future towns and cities. As Thomas Cahill points out, the monasteries founded by Irish monks "would become in time the cities of Lumieges, Auxerre, Laon, Luxeuil, Liege, Trier, Wurzburg, Regensburg, Rheinau, Reichenau, Salzburg, Vienna, Saint Gall, Bobbio, Fiesole and Lucca, to name but a few."[13] As Janet Nelson asserts: "In the early middle ages it was the churches, episcopal and monastic, which provided the major, if not quite the only, foci for town life."[14] Nothing shows better the potential modern ecclesiastical "settlements" could have in our own day in helping repair our own fraying communal life, reverse the atomization of suburbia, and put the church back at the center of local community life.

Layout and Design of Monastic Settlements

One of the characteristics that set Irish monastic settlements apart was that many were ruled by women, abbesses who oversaw thriving communities of both men and women. One such abbess was Brigid, who founded probably the most famous monastic settlement in early medieval Ireland, Kildare. Overlooking the plain of

---

13. Cahill, *How the Irish Saved Civilization*, 194.
14. Blair, *Church in Anglo-Saxon Society*, 277.

The Early Irish Monastic Settlements

the nearby river Liffey, it became a hub of worship, learning, and metalwork. Cogitosus, a seventh century visitor to the settlement, portrays it thus:

> And who can describe in words the supreme beauty of this church, and the countless wonders of that minster (monasterium)—of that city (civitas) as we may say, if it can rightly be called a city when it is surrounded by no circuit of walls? But because countless peoples come together in it, it earns the name "city" from the gathering of crowds there. This city is supreme and metropolitan, in whose suburbs (suburbani), which holy Brigit marked out with a precise boundary (certo limite designavit), is feared no mortal adversary nor onslaught of enemies. But it is the safest city of refuge, with all its external suburbs (cum suis omnibus deforis suburbanis), in the whole land of the Irish for all fugitives. Treasures of kings are kept there . . . And who can count the varied crowds and countless peoples flocking together from all provinces? Some come because of the abundance of feasts, others to obtain healing of their ailments, others to stare at the crowds; others bring great gifts and offerings to the celebration of holy Brigit's birth.[15]

But what did such monastic settlements look like? And what can we learn from their layout and composition that might be helpful in creating our own, contemporary monastic settlements? The Irish laid out their monastic settlements as concentric zones around a holy core, patterned after the vision of the idealized temple found in Ezek 40–48.[16]

> This biblical conception of zones around a holy centre, combined with the rather different one of "refuge cities" for accidental killers, produced an ideal image of the holy city at the heart of graded precincts.[17]

---

15. Swift, "Forts and Fields," 105.
16. Blair, *Church in Anglo-Saxon Society*, 221.
17. Blair, *Church in Anglo-Saxon Society*, 222.

Building the Benedict Option

The architectural hierarchy implied in such a layout ensured that the church building lay at the center of the community.[18]

George Hunter describes what Cogitosus and other visitors would have seen as they entered such a settlement:

> *The visitor would first pass through a circular outer wall and through a gate that signified one was entering hallowed ground. The wall did not signify an enclosure to keep out the world; the area signified an "alternative" way of life, free of aggression and violence and devoted to God's purpose, that the community modelled for the world. . . . Once past the enclosure the visitor (as at Glendalough) would notice a porter's dwelling, a cathedral, several chapels, a round tower, one or more tall stone Celtic crosses, a cemetery, a well, the abbot's house, a guesthouse, many small cells for one or two people, large dwellings for families, a kitchen, refectory, a scriptorium, a library, workshops, farmland, and grazing land.*[19]

The Irish Christianity of late antiquity possessed a vision of church not truncated by the idea that the world was divided into secular and non-secular spheres. Faith had not yet retreated into the cramped space of personal pietistic devotion, but rather spoke to all life; in the words of Gerard Manley Hopkins it recognized that "all things . . . are charged with love, are charged with God."[20] Christ was Lord over every square inch of space and, therefore, the church itself provided the canopy under which all life was lived.

A Holistic Faith

Irish monks evangelized Europe and embodied their Christian faith through the physical organization of their communities. And because they believed the gospel spoke to all of life, their settlements included a multiplicity of buildings related to all areas of life: worship, living, work, hospitality, and education. Therefore,

---

18. Swift, *Church in Anglo-Saxon Society*, 118.
19. Hunter, *Celtic Way of Evangelism*, 17–18.
20. Nixon and Barber, *Collected Works of Gerard Manley Hopkins*, 471.

our proposed Ben Op community, informed by the model of the early Irish monastic communities, will include places to live, work, play, learn, and worship. By doing so, we will be building in a way characteristic of all traditional urban neighborhoods. As Léon Krier, the most influential traditional urbanist of our time, puts it:

> *A neighborhood is to the larger city what a slice of pizza is to the whole pie: a part that contains within itself the essential qualities and elements of the whole . . . this means that a neighborhood contains within walkable proximity to one another places to live, work, play, learn and worship.*[21]

Such a holistic development explicitly pushes back against modern society's relegation of Christianity to a truncated, private faith, huddled in a defensive crouch, and reaffirms that Christ is Lord over all, and therefore the church speaks to all aspects of life. It reaffirms that, as the church, we are called to be a colony of heaven living out our life here on Earth according to the value system of the age to come. Or, in the words of Gordon Fee, "We are the people of the future, living out the life of the future, here on earth in the present."[22]

But what specifically would this look like? Philip Bess points the way. In his book *Till We Have Built Jerusalem*, he lays out a proposal:

> *Beginning in 17th century London, small city, aristocratic estate-holders would contract with a developer to build, on a six- to ten-acre parcel of land, a square surrounded by housing, and in a few cases fronted by a parish church. This happened around the outskirts of London for a period of about two hundred years . . . . My proposition is this: Christian communities today should consider taking a development role analogous to the London aristocrat. Instead of building a church and a parking lot on our typical six to fifteen suburban acres, why could we not make a church building, a public (not private) square, perhaps*

---

21. Bess, *Till We Have Built Jerusalem*, 117.

22. From a public lecture by Gordon Fee at the Center for Christian Study, Charlottesville, Virginia, 1987.

> *school, and the beginnings of a mixed-use neighborhood? Why couldn't a church partner with a developer and use some of the proceeds from the development of its property to pay for part of the construction of its church building? Why couldn't churches use this strategy to begin to integrate housing and commercial buildings into suburbia as part of mixed-use neighborhoods? And who's to say that an initially random proliferation of such developments across suburbia over time might not become as it did in London, the very physical and spiritual centers so pointedly lacking in contemporary suburbia?*[23]

In the following chapters we will make a case for the specific buildings such a settlement should contain and why such buildings serve to nurture the life of Christian community, support effective outreach, and help repair the social fabric of the broader community.

---

23. Bess, *Till We Have Built Jerusalem*, 131.

The Early Irish Monastic Settlements

Diagram of 660-feet-by-660-feet (ten-acre) parcel with church, school, a variety of housing, retail space, plaza, square, and parking for nearly four hundred cars. Drawing by Elizabeth Ruedisale McNicholas, courtesy of Thursday Associates.

My chief goal, as stated above, is to provide a template for those contemplating church construction. More specifically, I want to encourage them not to construct a stand-alone building, but rather to conceive of a church building that is part of a more comprehensive development. Therefore, it seems appropriate that the first building we discuss should be that of the church . . . .

Chapter 3

The Church Building
Encouraging an Upward Gaze

It is long past the time to get rid of everything ugly and stupid from our churches, most of it visited upon them since the great iconoclasm of the sixties, and return to genuine art that stirs the imagination and pleases the eye, that entices with beauty— even sometimes a dread beauty—before a single word of a sermon is uttered.

—Anthony Esolen, *Out of the Ashes*

Dear Pilgrims of France, look upon this cathedral! Your ancestors built it to proclaim their faith! Everything, in its architecture, its sculpture, its windows, proclaims the joy of being saved and loved by God. Your ancestors were not perfect, they were not without sins. But they wanted to let the light of faith illuminate their darkness!

—Cardinal Sarah, *Homily to Chartres Pilgrims*

Bibles in Stone

Rod Dreher grew up in a town of two thousand on the Mississippi river in Louisiana, in a family of hunters and fishermen with a distrust of big-city intellectuals. As a very young boy, he would walk to the end of a pecan orchard where his two aunts, Lois and Hilda, lived in a little pre-Civil War cabin. Born in the 1890s, the two elderly ladies had led an adventurous life. They would sit for what seemed like hours on a red leather sofa, while their little nephew sat between them, chubby legs dangling, looking at a photo album from their time in France during the Great War. Rod was enraptured by their stories of far distant places and even as a young boy developed a desire to travel, a desire that only increased as he grew older.

Some years later, in 1984, Dreher's mother won a trip to Europe in a church raffle. She didn't want to go, but knew her seventeen-year-old son did. In short order the Louisiana teen found himself to be the only young person on a bus of elderly American tourists winding its way across Europe. The bus stopped an hour outside of Paris to see what, Rod thought at the time, would be "another old church." Though not particularly interested, he tagged along after the group, and entered Chartres Cathedral, one of the most glorious cathedrals in the West. There was nothing in his life or background growing up in a small Southern town that prepared him for, as he puts it, "the glory of God made manifest in that medieval cathedral." Speaking of that moment, Dreher recounts:

> I remember standing right in the middle of the labyrinth there, looking up at the rose window and all around . . . I realized God exists, and not only did He exist, but that He wants me. I remember thinking I want to know the kind of Christianity that could inspire men, the names of whom we don't even know, to build such a temple to the glory of its God.[1]

As Dreher puts it:

> I had never imagined that Christianity could produce a building so beautiful. Being present in this medieval cathedral made me desperately want to know the God that had inspired men to build such a temple to his honor.[2]

Beauty, Verticality, and Awe

The Irish understood the power of architecture to create a sense of awe, draw one's thoughts to the divine, and express key theological truths. The church at Kildare was the prime example of such tendencies. It possessed a high roof, spacious floor, and three separate areas partitioned by walls and hangings. On either side of the ornate altar, encrusted with gold, silver, and gems, stood the tombs of Saint Brigit and her bishop, Conlaed. A profusion of images and carvings of various colors surrounded the tombs while silver and gold chandeliers hung above and illuminated the tombs.[3] In addition, as Tomas Ó Carragáin points out:

> Worshippers were organized by rank and sex with separate spaces and entrances for each group. The geography of Kildare placed women to the north but allowed both male and female officials at Kildare into the sanctuary rhyming

1. Danube Institute, "Evening with Rod Dreher."
2. Tripkovic, "Columnist Rod Dreher Talks Orthodoxy," §5.
3. Bitel, *Ekphrasis at Kildare*, 616.

visually with the placement of Brigit on the north side of the sanctuary and Conlaed to her south. The segregation of females to the north from males to the south was not uncommon in Christian churches and theologically echoed other dualities: Old Testament and New, dark and light, moon and sun. Mosaics and paintings to the north were normally of female saints . . . while southern walls featured male saints. Cogitosus' divisions operated in time as well as space, in liturgy as well as architecture.[4]

"The geography of the two saints' burials [put them at the center of all ceremonies] and mirrored the social and moral hierarchy of Brigit's parishioners and Christian communities generally."[5]

Even the much smaller and more numerous parish churches the Irish constructed may have been built in such a way as to encourage a sense of awe and devotion. Constructed of dry stone with only two windows, Tomas Ó Carragáin describes them thus:

> In the case of the Irish churches it is almost as if those commissioning them were aiming to create an atmosphere that was as different as possible from the outdoors, or indeed the relatively flimsy domestic buildings of the day, perhaps to heighten the sense that one was entering a sacred, almost otherworldly space. The coldness of the stone walls and the dimly seen but massive beams of the roof above would have contributed to this, as would carefully positioned lighting, through which certain focal points were illuminated in the gloom. . . . In good weather, the thin shafts of sunlight projected by the unnecessarily small windows were undoubtedly the strongest sources of light in the church; and it would make sense if this light fell on the most important focal point: the altar or perhaps the priest as he consecrated the host just west of the altar.[6]

Although in much popular movie culture churches are invariably shown, like the church at Kildare, with all the trappings of sacred architectural elements, the days of the white clapboard

---

4. Bitel, *Ekphrasis at Kildare*, 621
5. Bitel, *Ekphrasis at Kildare*, 617.
6. Carragáin, "Architectural Setting of the Mass," 133.

church with stained glass windows and a steepled cross are long gone. Most churches built in the past fifty years draw their inspiration from the mall and the business office. They are largely indistinguishable from the undifferentiated suburban landscape that prevails in much of America today, untethered from any sense of tradition, history, or culture. Where churches are not merely bland, they assault one with an almost visceral ugliness. We send a message about the God we worship through the churches we build. They are Bibles in stone that by their very shape reveal our conception of the God we worship.

Big Bland Boxes

In contrast to the sublime architecture of Chartres Cathedral, whose beauty left a young Louisiana teenager stunned and shaken, most church architecture today is meant to anesthetize, to make us comfortable in our modern American sensibilities. Far from drawing our thoughts upward and confronting us with the reality of a divine universe and a God who calls forth a response from us, it inures us to our modern, suburban, capitalistic, and self-referential existence.

Photo taken by the author.

As Greg Dickinson puts it:

The Church Building

Rather than creating a church set apart from the world, these are churches that are resolutely, even dogmatically, of the world. They [modern megachurches] are absolutely connected to the popular culture that surrounds them. They do not just speak to or about popular consumer culture; instead they speak with and through popular consumer culture. Everything about the buildings embodies comfort and security, nothing speaks to sacrifice or change or distinctiveness. Ahistorical and devoid of references to previous church forms, the mega church's architecture is a blank slate on which church communities can write their late modern, high technology, consumerist identities.[7]

But why? What has served to bring about this sea change in church architecture? What has driven the almost complete rejection of historic forms of sacred architecture on the part of Evangelicalism? In part, the mistaken assumption that such traditional "church" architectural elements were a barrier to the unchurched attending church. As former megachurch pastor Bill Hybels put it:

What I want [the un-churched visitor] to do is just say, "I was just at corporate headquarters for IBM in Atlanta Wednesday, and now I come to church and it's basically the same." Neutrality, comfort, contemporary, clean: Those are the kinds of values that we want to communicate.[8]

It is not an exaggeration to say that Hybels's view became the guiding principle for most new church construction over the past thirty to forty years. As Dr. Matthew Niermann explains:

Over the past several decades Evangelical Protestant churches have sought to build buildings that differ from traditional church architecture in order to attract unchurched individuals to the church. . . . This missions-based theory of church design is known as architectural evangelism. It proposes that traditional church architecture acts as a barrier for the unchurched and thus churches should build buildings rooted in secular typologies, using few or no ecclesiological markers, and constructed with low-cost

---

7. Dickinson, *Suburban Dreams*, 141, 150.
8. Dickinson, *Suburban Dreams*, 135–36.

materials. Familiar with this kind of building, [the thinking goes] the unchurched will be more apt to attend.[9]

But contrary to such popular beliefs, recent research has in fact shown that traditional church architecture is more appealing to the unchurched than a more modern, anodyne approach. Specifically:

> Both Barna Research Group's Making Space for Millennials *and* Lifeway Research Group's "Sacred Space" *concluded that [the unchurched] preferred more prototypical or traditional churches over secular-based churches. . . . Unchurched individuals are not primarily driven by perception of comfort, nor do they prefer churches designed with non-prototypical secular based modern forms. Rather, they, like churched individuals, are primarily motivated and drawn to perceptions of beauty—which are best understood as churches designed with prototypical form, including strong use of ecclesiological elements, sloped roofs, and pre-modern and mixed compositional hierarchies.*[10]

And a new British-based study, looking at conversion among young people in the Church of England, found that:

> *The "influence of a church building was more significant than attending a youth group, going to a wedding, or speaking to other Christians about their faith." In fact, "The study suggests that new methods invested in by the church, such as youth groups . . . are less effective than prayer or visiting a church building in attracting children to the church."*[11]

Recent work by Ann Sussman and Justin B. Hollander, using eye tracking technology, highlights just why people may have a preference for older traditional forms of architecture over modern architecture. Such eye tracking software has enabled us to see how

---

9. Niermann, "Comfort or Beauty?," §1–2.
10. Niermann, "Comfort or Beauty?," §3, 38.
11. Kosloski, "New Study," §3–4.

people react to different types of architecture, and reveals that, as Sussman points out:

> Traditional buildings, pre-twentieth century, [are] implicitly easy for viewers to take in, and approachable, while post-twentieth-century architectural buildings are the reverse: harder to focus on and avoidant.[12]

It appears that because of the way our brains are hard-wired, they easily and consistently fixate on traditional and vernacular architecture, while avoiding modern architecture with its blank facades and steel superstructures. Based on these considerations, when considering an architectural style for new church construction, it would seem best to build in a traditional style.

If traditional church architecture is to be preferred, then, what are its characteristics? Philip Bess explains:

> Broadly speaking, virtually all sacred architecture prior to about 1950 exhibits some or all of the following six characteristics: A recognizable verticality, in either or both height and depth; A concern for light and shadow; A care for craft, durability and material particularity; The conscious use of mathematics and geometry as formal ordering devices; A compositional and artistic unity; and, A sense of hierarchy, i.e. formal evidence in the architecture itself that some forms and what they represent are regarded as more important than others.[13]

---

12. Sussman and Hollander, *Cognitive Architecture*, 178–79.
13. Bess, *Till We Have Built Jerusalem*, 34–35.

Beyond including these general characteristics, it would seem best to allow the design to be guided by the specific local context in which the church is built. For instance, one may want the church to conform to traditional historic styles of a particular geographic region, e.g., a church located in Arizona may want to reflect the adobe style common to the Southwest. Such an approach seeks to counteract the ahistorical nature of most new development and instead roots it in a local, historical tradition.

Another option would be to follow a traditional American architectural style such as the Craftsman movement of the late nineteenth and early twentieth century. It is a truly domestic style of American architecture that emphasized durability, craftsmanship, and simplicity. In addition, while anecdotal, currently there seems to be somewhat of a resurgence of interest in it among builders.

In any event, regardless of what architectural style is chosen, it is helpful to keep in mind Dorothy Sayers's admonition that:

> *No piety in the worker will compensate for the work that is not true to itself. For any work that is untrue to its own*

technique is a living lie. Yet in her own buildings, in her own ecclesiastical art and music, in her hymns and prayers, in her sermons and in her little book of devotions, the church will tolerate or permit a pious intention to excuse work so ugly, so pretentious, so tawdry, and twaddling, so insincere, and insipid, so bad as to shock and horrify any decent draftsman. . . . She has forgotten that a building must be good architecturally before it can be a good church. That a painting must be well painted before it can be a sacred picture, that a work must be a good work before it can call itself God's work.[14]

---

14. Sayers, "Why Work?," 115.

Chapter 4

Housing
Rebuilding the Neighborhood

You do not feel comfortable sending your child outdoors to play. Of course you don't. You have no neighborhood, only a geographical area. You have no local school. You do not know any of the mothers nearby. Old people live far away. Everyone is indoors or in a sports corral somewhere. Small businesses are gone. Responsible people are never to be seen, because they are at work. . . . The older people do not play cards with one another. No one visits anyone. Hospitality—your home's openness to anyone who might show up at the door, any day, any hour—is a thing of the past.

—Anthony Esolen, *Out of the Ashes*

The Housing Crisis

> It is morning in Eastern Housing Court, and Frances Louis is seated on a bench in the gallery of a courtroom, waiting for her case to be called. Outwardly, she appears calm, given the gravity of the case, but later she will admit to having "a headache that won't quit." Her landlord is trying to evict her

from her Roxbury home of 12 years, where she lives with her parents, both in their 70s, and three adult children. . . . Using her walker, Louis approaches the attorney tables, flanked by several relatives and her attorneys. The landlord wants to increase the rent for her three-bedroom on Cobden Street from $1,685 to $3,550, something Louis, who is on disability with congestive heart failure, cannot afford.[1]

Louis is the face of a national housing crisis that is currently gripping America. A recent study found that "Americans earning less than $100,000 annually . . . now struggle to afford a median-priced home." This is a more than 50 percent jump since 2021, when the average American only needed $73,668 in annual income to meet a similar threshold.[2] As a result, according to the Urban Land Institute, there is an increasing segment of the population that spends more than 30 percent of their income on housing, thus reducing their purchasing power for other amenities.[3] Janneke Ratcliffe of the Urban Institute predicts that the US is in need of roughly 3.8 million to 5.5 million more housing units, primarily geared toward low- and moderate-income families and first-time homebuyers.[4] It's hard to overemphasize the financial pressure and accompanying emotional turmoil experienced by an increasing number of Americans who can't find decent, affordable housing.

1. McDonald, "'I'm at My Wit's End.'"
2. Blaff, "Six Figure Income Now Required," §1–3.
3. Urban Land Institute, *What's Next?*
4. Ratcliffe, "How We Can Solve," §1–2.

One fairly recent phenomenon that may be contributing to higher housing costs is the advent of large private investment firms into the housing market. Firms such as BlackRock have begun to buy up vast quantities of single-family houses to turn into rental units. According to Bradley Devlin, one-quarter of recent home purchases in Houston were by billionaire investor Larry Fink. This influx of massive capital into the housing market inflates prices and pushes out individual buyers who can't compete with large corporations. Fink, BlackRock, and other firms are thus doing their part to create a permanent renter class.[5]

Another likely factor contributing to our current crisis is the absence of what has come to be called "missing middle" housing. For almost the past one hundred years, the zoning code in the United States has privileged two types of dwellings: single-family houses and large apartment/condo buildings. As Daniel Parolek points out:

> Missing Middle [housing] contains all of the housing types in-between the single-family and the larger apartment and condo buildings: Duplex, Triplex, the Cottage Court, that used to be an inherent part of our neighborhood fabric that we just stopped building several decades ago.[6]

This lack of options has exacerbated the affordable housing crisis because many people cannot afford a large, single-family house, and most residents of existing neighborhoods don't want large apartment buildings destroying their neighborhood and thus block such construction. As Parolek puts it:

> Current zoning has allowed a lot of really bad, ugly, unattractive, incompatible infill in neighborhoods, and . . . given density a really bad name, multi-family a bad name, and the concepts of apartments [a bad name].[7]

Therefore, people are priced out of single-family homes while being unable to find available apartments.

5. Devlin, "BlackRock Plots to Buy Ukraine."
6. Parolek, "Missing Middle Housing."
7. Parolek, "Missing Middle Housing."

Housing

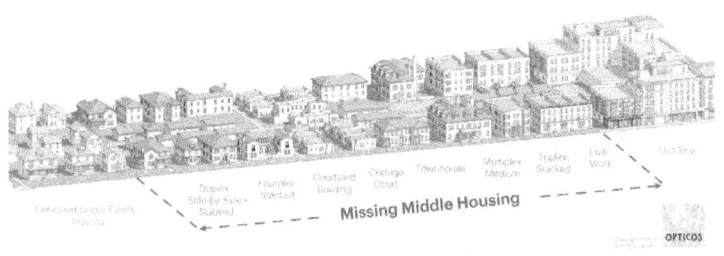

Missing Middle Housing concept created by Daniel Parolek; for more info visit www.missingmiddlehousing.com (Image © Opticos Design, Inc.)

These are but two of the many issues that may be contributing to our current housing crisis. But as with many of the pressing issues of our day, the church seems to have largely been absent. An enormous amount of money has been spent over the past forty years to construct large, isolated churches sitting alone in seas of asphalt—churches that sit vacant most of the week and do little to ameliorate the current housing crisis. In contrast, Irish monastic communities included various types of housing along with their church building. Why? Because (as already stated), rather than being composed of a handful of cloistered monks, they included large groups of people, both lay and ordained, representing a variety of occupations and ages. Because of this, housing would by necessity have comprised a significant part of any such settlement (usually taking the form of *clocháns*, drystone, beehive shaped huts).

Ben Op communities will be no different. By broadening the type of buildings constructed, particularly those with nineteen or fewer units (i.e., missing middle housing), greater density will be possible providing housing at a greater range of prices. Instead of building stand-alone churches, Ben Op communities will offer a variety of housing, including single-family houses, fourplexes, apartments, and row homes (the mix of housing offered will depend on the amount of land available). This will provide a variety of housing tailored to fit people at different life stages: singles, families with children, and young professionals. In addition, by reserving a certain percentage of units for the working poor and senior citizens, an even broader community will be encouraged with genuine economic and demographic diversity. Ben Op communities will thus help address the current housing crisis while helping repair the broader social fabric.

The particular mix of such homes will depend on the demographics of the community in which a monastic settlement is being built and the availability of land. In areas of higher density and less available land, a settlement might focus more on mixed middle housing and row houses. If a church has more acreage, the mixing of housing provided might include single-family homes. This also means that when arriving at your particular mix of housing, you'll need to be sensitive to the market demands in your particular community. This means that you'll need to analyze the demographic data for your community. The good news is that such information is readily available from a variety of sources: US Census data can be accessed online, many counties and municipalities have such data on their homepage, and there are many companies that, for a modest fee, will produce a demographic study for you.

Fostering Community by Design

But how should such houses be laid out? It is here that Christopher Alexander offers helpful guidance. In his book *A Pattern Language: Towns, Building, Construction*, Alexander and a team of researchers lay out guidelines for planning modern communities based on patterns of design inherent in traditional communities. Such patterns have arisen organically over the years as a result of the way people respond to and interact with their built environment and thus encourage both community and human flourishing. Alexander recommends building housing in what he calls "housing clusters": "rough but identifiable clusters of 8 to 12 households around some common land."[8] As Ross Chapin points out:

> [Traditionally], villages and towns nearly always had gathering places for the community—the village green,

8. Alexander et al., *Pattern Language*, 277.

town square, market street, pub, church—that served the needs for economic, social and religious exchange.[9]

The Irish monastic settlements followed this same principle, by having the atrium (or platea): "an area of open access by the entire community that formed a focus for communal activities."[10]

This principle of having a central common space is almost totally lacking in the design of most suburbs with the result that, as mentioned earlier, modern neighborhoods are "merely collections of individual houses, each an island in itself, with little real connection among neighbors."[11] But, as Ross Chapin explains, a common space can go along way toward building a sense of community in almost any neighborhood:

> With a centrally located green space or commons, in lieu of a street down the middle, and with a clearly and elegantly demarcated entrance into the neighborhood, a collective identity is created.[12] . . . Shared outdoor space is a key element. . . . It is neither private (home, yard) nor public (a busy street, park) but rather a defined space between the private and public realms. . . . Because of its location and design, the shared outdoor space fosters casual interaction among neighbors, which, in time, may grow into deeper, long-term friendships.[13]

Such common land allows people to feel comfortable outside their own homes and part of a larger social system, while providing a natural meeting place for neighbors.

Over the past decade, there has been a growing recognition of this dynamic among architects and planners, resulting in the proliferation of what are called "pocket neighborhoods": clusters of usually not more than ten to sixteen houses sharing a common, landscaped piece of land. Such a development/arrangement was not uncommon in America in the late nineteenth and early

---

9. Chapin, *Pocket Neighborhoods*, 19.
10. Swift, "Forts and Fields," 111.
11. Chapin, *Pocket Neighborhoods*, 7.
12. Chapin, *Pocket Neighborhoods*, 5.
13. Chapin, *Pocket Neighborhoods*, 8.

twentieth centuries, with the cottage court being one example of such a design. But as in so much else relating to architecture and urban planning today, a new generation is having to relearn concepts once widely known by past generations.

Missing Middle Housing concept created by Daniel Parolek; for more info visit www.missingmiddlehousing.com (Image © Opticos Design, Inc.)

As well as building a sense of community and thus social capital, a central commons plays another important role in the overall mental health and well-being of residents: it provides access to nature or, as it is sometimes called, "green space." Layla McCay, author of *Restorative Cities: Urban Design for Mental Health Wellbeing*, explains:

> Ample research tells us [that access to green space] can reduce depression, stress, it can improve brain function, it can help manage the symptoms and severity of anxiety disorders, of schizophrenia, of HDAD, of dementia, plus,

green urban space can help to reduce heat stress and improve sleep quality, which are both really important for supporting people's mental health.[14]

Put bluntly, "To stay healthy, everyone needs some green. . . . Environmentally deprived people fare worse than those in greener surroundings."[15] The positive effects of such green space are dependent on a number of factors, including the proximity to one's residence. By making such a commons the central part of any modern monastic community, green space is placed literally right outside residents' doors, thus supporting their physical and mental well-being. Therefore, a key element of any Ben Op community will be a piece of common land shared by a "house cluster."

Another potential element of such a cluster is what Christopher Alexander refers to as a "Main Gateway." Alexander explains:

> House clusters get their identity most clearly from the fact that you pass through a definite gateway to enter them—it is this gateway acting as a threshold which creates the unit. . . . A gateway can have many forms: a literal gate, a bridge, a passage between narrowly separated buildings, an

14. Roe and McCay, "Author's Forum on Urbanism."
15. Klinenberg, *Palaces for the People*, 145.

avenue of trees, a gateway through a building. All of them have the same function: they mark a point where a path crosses a boundary and help maintain the boundary.[16]

So key elements of a fully developed Ben Op community would include a church with a house cluster around a commons with a "gateway." But if housing is to be part of any Ben Op community, what style of homes should be built?

Architecture, Symmetry, and Biometrics

As with our discussion on church architectural styles, drawing on recent biometric studies, Sussman and Hollander provide guidance. In their book *Cognitive Architecture*, they remark on people's innate propensity to find human faces in objects (a phenomenon called *pareidolia*, and one understood and utilized by car makers and other manufacturers). As they put it:

> *Our face-sensing capability is so strong and present that faces also appear to be put into building elevations or facades unintentionally. It reflects the fact that some researchers believe that pareidolia, the subconscious tendency to assemble faces in random objects, plays a much more significant role in design, aesthetics, and our appreciations of buildings and cityscapes than is generally realized.*[17]

In addition, Sussman and Hollander highlight the fact that human beings seem to have a natural disposition toward symmetry. They point out that we process symmetrical designs more quickly than nonsymmetrical ones and that "researchers have learned that looking at symmetrical objects subconsciously activates our smiling muscles more than looking at random patterns. And when we smile, we are more likely to feel calm or reassured."[18]

Therefore, in choosing an architectural style for housing it seems best to a choose a traditional style that precludes more

---

16. Alexander et. al., *Pattern Language*, 277.
17. Sussman and Hollander, *Cognitive Architecture*, 67.
18. Sussman and Hollander, *Cognitive Architecture*, 110.

modern designs such as ranch and split-level homes. This would also ensure a degree of continuity between the church building and the housing units.

These considerations also bear on the layout of the houses themselves vis-à-vis the church. As with Philip Bess's proposal, housing units surrounding a square provide a perfect symmetrical framing for the church, helping to highlight its specific qualities. In addition to the particular architectural style to adopt, there are two other elements to be considered: porches and parking.

The Importance of Porches

The technology we use shapes us, often in ways of which we're unaware. The almost complete absence of porches on many modern homes is one of the clearest examples of this fact (where a porch *is* present, it is often largely ornamental, being too small to be of any practical use). My mother grew up in a tiny row house in Richmond, Virginia. One of her most vivid childhood memories is of her parents, after the dinner table was cleared, going out to sit on their front porch swing. As they watched the cherry red glow of the sunset ebb away, they would talk over the news of the day with their neighbors who were sitting on their front porch (only a small alley separated the houses). This was a common occurrence of many in the US prior to the fifties and sixties and it was one of the myriad ways in which a strong sense of community was fostered in the neighborhoods of that day.

With the invention of air-conditioning, however, and the accompanying growth to prominence of the television set, families increasingly began to stay inside. Builders responded accordingly and, beginning in the fifties, homes increasingly lacked a front porch. The inadvertent result was to discourage the social interaction that had taken place naturally when neighbors spent time on their front porches, thus serving to lower social capital and increase the growing atomization of American life. Therefore, when building housing units as part of a Ben Op community, when at all possible, housing should include porches opening onto the shared commons.

The Problem with Parking

As with porches, garages are another visible reminder of the way technology has adversely affected our built environment and so served to undermine social capital. With the rise of the automobile, increasingly houses were constructed in such a way that garages project out from the front of the house and connect to it. Presumably this was meant to minimize, as much as possible, the time required to travel from the sealed interior of one's car to the sealed interior of one's house, while minimizing any potential contact with neighbors. This trend thus served not only to destroy the natural symmetry of houses and undermine community, it encroached upon the land available in the front yard for use by the family. As a result, when they were outside, families increasingly chose to spend time in the backyard—thus further serving to undermine a sense of neighborhood cohesion. To drive through a modern suburb today is to drive past a façade of seemingly empty homes, devoid of human life. What life is present is safely tucked away in backyards out of sight. Therefore, to further encourage the social interaction in the common area of a Ben Op community, whenever possible, parking should be in the back of housing units, hidden as much as possible from the commons while still being accessible to residents.

Further Thoughts on Parking

Because over the past fifty years we have designed our communities to be car-centric and neglected a viable public transportation system, today most new construction, particularly non-residential, requires an inordinate amount of parking. In essence this is wasted space or, as Christopher Alexander puts it, "Vast parking lots wreck the land for people."[19] However, since parking will inevitably be a part of any Ben Op, when building it seems best to consider the guidelines suggested by Alexander:

> Parked cars ... can ... be distributed in two entirely different ways. They can be concentrated in a few huge parking lots; or they can be scattered in many tiny parking lots. The tiny parking lots are far better for the environment than the large ones, even when their total areas are the same. Make parking lots small, serving no more than five to seven cars, each surrounded by garden walls, hedges, fences, slopes and trees, so that from the outside the cars

---

19. Alexander et al., *Pattern Language*, 506.

are almost invisible. Space these small lots so that they are at least 100 feet apart.[20]

Obviously, Alexander describes the ideal situation, one in which there is sufficient acreage to allow such dispersed parking. It may not be feasible for many developments.

The one building of the Ben Op that will require the most parking, by far, is the church building. The number of parking spaces required by your local zoning ordinances will vary by municipality, but the most common ratio of congregation members to parking spots is four to one or three to one. This means that a church with a sanctuary holding four hundred people will require one hundred parking slots. Unlike the parking for your housing, which ideally will be dispersed, your church parking will most likely have to be consolidated and adjacent to the church. There are several possible ways to lessen the size of the parking lot required, however. One way is to construct a smaller sanctuary, too small to seat the entire congregation, and then hold multiple services. This allows for a more efficient use of the church building, while leaving more land available for housing, the commons, and other

---

20. Alexander et al., *Pattern Language*, 504.

components of the settlement. Another potential way to reduce the size of church parking is to build near a public road that provides on-street parking. And finally, some leeway may be permitted by your municipality regarding the parking ratio if a significant percentage of the congregation is composed of residents of the Ben Op itself, and so can walk to church.

Rental Income: Expanding Your Financial Base

One very real benefit from including housing is that, rather than spending money on a building that will immediately become a financial drain, a congregation will be investing in buildings that will provide a funding stream that can be used to support the life of the congregation, hire staff, and support its mission to the broader community. In doing so, we'll be following the example of the Irish. By making space for and cultivating various trades in their monastic settlements, they not only helped strengthen the local economy in which they were located, but, more to our point, they provided the church with income it could use to minister to those in need as well as finance missionary teams in their work of founding new monastic settlements.

All this having been said, it is very important, when considering a venture that includes housing, that you take the time upfront to really crunch the numbers to see if your plan is viable. Determining whether the housing component of your Ben Op is fiscally viable will involve such things as determining the difference between your estimated monthly income from your properties and the expected monthly expenses of that housing. This is your net operating income or NOI. Another piece of key information needed in determining financial viability is the estimate of the cash flow from your rental property.

All this may sound somewhat daunting, particularly for church leaders unacquainted with the business world. This is where developing a relationship with a local builder you trust and who shares your values is absolutely essential. Such a developer can help you assess the financial viability of any housing plan as well as develop that plan. In addition, an easy answer to the dilemma of managing your property is to hire a property management company. In fact, it's not unusual for churches to have congregational members with management experience who could work part-time and be paid through the rental income brought in by the properties themselves.

Many churches today operate within a very small margin of fiscal viability. If some of the broad cultural trends continue (as they most likely will), or if the federal government should ever enact legislation affecting the faith-based community (e.g., repealing faith-based organizations' tax-exempt status), many churches would become fiscally unsustainable overnight. One of the advantages of the type of approach being argued for here is that it broadens the potential funding stream of a congregation, while increasing its resilience and ability to weather potential shocks. What is almost certainly assured is that the church will need to begin to think outside of the box in the years ahead if it is to weather the storms gathering on the horizon. The approach proposed here is one possible way of its doing so.

Chapter 5

Amenities
Providing Social Infrastructure

When you build a thing you cannot merely build that thing in isolation, but must also repair the world around it, and within it, so that the larger world at that one place becomes more coherent, and more whole; and the thing which you make takes its place in the web of nature, as you make it.

—CHRISTOPHER ALEXANDER, *A PATTERN LANGUAGE*

We shape our buildings, and afterwards our buildings shape us.

—WINSTON CHURCHILL,
OCTOBER 28, 1943, HOUSE OF COMMONS

Social Infrastructure

My wife and I live in a large planned community in the Washington, DC, area. Our townhome stands across the street from several tennis courts, a basketball court, a playground, and outside exercise bars. While most of the community remains relatively deserted at night, with occasional walkers ambling through empty streets, this area is a hive of activity both in the evenings and on weekends: laughter drifting across the street from energetic groups playing pickleball or tennis, shouted encouragements from those playing on the basketball court, and shrieks of glee from children playing on the playground. We are seeing first-hand the importance of what planners call social infrastructure for the health of a community, and it is one of the reasons Irish monastic settlements were so effective at building social cohesion and developing community. What is social infrastructure, and how does it contribute to the overall health of a community?

AMENITIES

In his book *Palaces for the People*, Eric Klinenberg has defined social infrastructure as:

> The physical conditions that determine whether social capital develops. Social infrastructure includes public institutions such as libraries, playgrounds and parks; community organizations that have physical gathering spaces such as churches; and "third spaces" such as cafes and other commercial establishments.[1]

Irish monastic settlements included a smithy, kitchens, a primary school, often multiple churches, a scriptorium, residential housing, and a hostel. They thus provided the social infrastructure necessary to foster and support a level of community unheard of in today's atomized culture. Residents of monastic settlements in the course of their everyday life were constantly running into each other. As George Hunter III points out:

> Within the threefold division of the day into worship, study, and work, monastic communities were beehives of a wide range of activities. . . . With some variation from one community to another, children went to school, young men and women prepared for Christian vocations, and Christian scholarship was fostered. Some inhabitants copied decaying books onto new parchments, others "illuminated" the Scriptures, and others practiced other arts and crafts. Other people herded cows, sheared sheep, made cloth, cultivated crops, cooked for the community, or cared for sick people, sick animals or guests.[2]

Thus, Irish monastic communities possessed a social infrastructure that played a key role in building the sense of community that made them so appealing to an early medieval culture that was increasingly marked by violence and mistrust. As Klinenberg points out:

> When social infrastructure is robust, it fosters contact, mutual support, and collaboration among friends and

---

1. Klinenberg, *Palaces for the People*, 5.
2. Hunter, *Celtic Way of Evangelism*, 17.

neighbors; when degraded, it inhibits social activity, leaving families and individuals to fend for themselves. Social infrastructure is crucially important, because local face-to-face interactions—at the school, the playground, the diner—are the building blocks of all public life. People forge bonds in places that have healthy social infrastructure—not because they set out to build community, but because when people engage in sustained, recurrent interaction, particularly while doing things they enjoy, relationships inevitably grow.[3]*

The Advantages of Amenities

Today, neighborhoods that provide social infrastructure in the form of various amenities provide numerous advantages to their residents. Ryan Streeter, in an article on the benefits of high amenity neighborhoods explains.

Amenities increase the desirability of houses and so your chance of selling/renting them.

> *Numerous studies show that people will pay more to be close to things they value when they're not at home or work. A study of nearly 100,000 home sales, for example, found a relationship between the ability to walk to neighborhood amenities and higher home values in 13 of 15 U.S. metro areas. In addition, a nationwide analysis in 2018 found a "walkability" premium in property values equal to an additional $28,000 on a $200,000 home.*[4]

Amenities increase the personal well-being of residents:

> *High-amenity urban dwellers are nearly four times as likely as low-amenity urban dwellers—37 percent versus 10 percent—to call their community an "excellent" place to live.... People in high-amenity neighborhoods are more likely to say they're happy, living the American dream, and*

---

3. Klinenberg, *Palaces for the People*, 5.
4. Streeter, "Wanted," §4.

Amenities

confident in their financial future. These characteristics pertain regardless of income or education level.[5]

In fact, recent research has shown that counties showing higher interactions at such third places fared better during COVID-19, seeing fewer personal bankruptcies, COVID-19 infections, and COVID-19 deaths.[6]

And finally, and most importantly for our purposes, amenities strengthen social cohesion and social capital:

> *Residents of amenity-rich urban neighborhoods . . . are twice as likely as those in lower-amenity areas to say that neighbors engage in reciprocity. . . . Living in higher-amenity neighborhoods is also associated with greater engagement and interest in broader community life. More than half of city and town residents with ample amenities report talking with neighbors about community happenings compared with about a quarter of those living in sparser places.*[7]

> *Trust is also considerably higher in well-rounded communities. Among urban residents, only those living in high-amenity neighborhoods say that most people can be trusted often. In moderate and low-amenity urban areas, large majorities say "one cannot be too careful" when asked about trust levels. And when it comes to trust at work and school, three-quarters of high-amenity residents say that they trust their colleagues compared with about half of those in lower amenity places.*[8]

In short:

> *The survey data confirm the import of having third places nearby for when Americans report that they have local amenities nearby that they visit regularly—such as a local coffee shop, bar, restaurant, gym, or park—most (58 percent), regardless of where they live, say that they feel close*

---

5. Streeter, "Wanted," §5, 8.
6. Makridis, "Social Capital and Covid."
7. Streeter, "Wanted," §6.
8. Streeter, "Wanted," §7.

Building the Benedict Option

to their neighborhoods and neighbors. The figure drops 15 points, to 43 percent, when they do not have a local third place to visit."[9]

So social infrastructure clearly plays an integral part in fostering community, and therefore will form an integral part of any Ben Op community. But what social infrastructure works best at creating community in twenty-first-century suburban America?

Appealing to Different Demographics

Because one goal of any Ben Op will be to create a community composed of a broad range of ages, it would seem best to offer amenities targeted to different groups. So for instance, building a basketball court would tend to target those seventeen and under (according to ESPN, basketball is the most popular youth team sport in America),[10] while offering a tennis court might serve to target an older demographic (61 percent of tennis players are thirty years or older).[11] In addition, with the rise in popularity of pickleball, a tennis court can do double duty, thus appealing to an even broader demographic.

9. Abrams, "What Are the Real Third Places?," §3.
10. Holmes, "These Kids Are Ticking Time Bombs."
11. Zippia, "Tennis Player Demographics."

One thing to consider when choosing what amenities to provide is the degree of upkeep they will require. So for instance, a basketball court might be a better choice over a pool that requires regular upkeep and staff. Also, keep in mind when considering what amenities to offer, that if you include housing as part of your Ben Op community, you'll be in competition for renters with other housing communities in your area, and so will need to offer at least as many, if not more, amenities as they do. So the range of amenities a Ben Op community provides might include the following:

- A playground to target families with small children
- One or more tennis courts to target older individuals
- A basketball court to appeal to youth and young adults
- A dog park to appeal to the sixty-two million households that own a dog[12]

Lowering Barriers through Community Involvement

One very important way to determine what amenities to provide, lower potential opposition from the surrounding community, and raise the likelihood of your project being approved by your local board of supervisors is to hold a charrette. What is a charrette? A charrette is a technique used by developers and urban planners to elicit input and involvement on the part of the broader community regarding a proposed development. In short, it's an opportunity for you to meet with local residents and municipal officials, share your general vision with them, and elicit their help in refining it to meet their specific needs. It's one of the most important ways you as a congregation can help assuage the fears of residents concerned about your church coming in and adversely affecting the character

---

12. This number will most likely increase. Increasingly, younger generations are putting off having children until later or opting not have children at all. Pets are increasingly taking the place of children among this demographic. (American Veterinary Medical Association, "2022 AVMA Pet Ownership and Demographics.")

of their neighborhood. Remember, how you build may be just as important as what you build in helping to strengthen social cohesion and capital in your community. It's also an integral part of our calling as the people of God to reflect his character and be peacemakers.

Chapter 6

The Coffee Shop
Third Spaces and Hospitality

Community is not something you have, like pizza. Nor is it something you can buy. It's a living organism based on a web of interdependencies—which is to say, a local economy. It expresses itself physically as connectedness, as buildings actively relating to each other, and to whatever public space exists, be it the street, or the courthouse or the village green.

—James Howard Kunstler, *Home from Nowhere*

Coffee, a Good Vibe, and Community

Ebenezer's Coffee Shop sits at the end of a tree-lined street of classic brick townhomes on the busy corner of 2nd and F Streets, a block from Union Station in Washington, DC. The original structure was a historic one-level diner built in 1908, with a brick addition added in 2005. If one walks in the door he or she is apt to be greeted by a friendly barista with short blond hair, quick to engage with customers and to talk about the difference her church has made in her life. When asked why they choose Ebenezer's customers give a variety of responses from the "nice vibe," to "good wifi," to "the sixteen ounce cups they offer (larger than the other coffee shop down the block)." Billed as "Coffee with a Cause" and boasting a performance space downstairs that hosts evangelistic Bible studies, Ebenezer's is owned by National Community Church. It is the fulfillment of their dream to create "a warm and convivial gatherings space . . . where the church and community could cross paths."[1] NCC is one of an increasing number of churches that are rediscovering the spiritual gift of hospitality, a gift the Irish understood well. A gift that found expression in the guest houses, or "*hospitiums*," they built.

Photo taken by the author.

1. National Community Church, "Ebenezer's Coffee House."

Hospitality

George Hunter points out that one of a "monastic community's highest commitments [was] hospitality to strangers, seekers, pilgrims, and refugees."[2] In his *History of the English Church and People*, the Venerable Bede records how many English nobles and lesser folk in the seventh century went to Ireland to study under various teachers and pursue a life of stricter discipline. "The [monks] welcomed them all kindly, and, without asking for any payment provided them with daily food, books and instruction."[3] By extending such hospitality to all comers, the Irish felt they were offering hospitality to Christ himself. Therefore, as Philip Sheldrake points out:

> *Guests . . . were accorded a kind of semi-spiritual status and housed within the sacred enclosure. Often the guest house was given the choicest site within the settlement and yet was always set apart, sometimes within its own enclosure. The hospitium, therefore, was within the sacred space (isolated from the outside world) yet separated from the monastic living quarters. The guest facility was itself, therefore, a kind of "boundary place" between two worlds.*[4]

As Richard Fletcher points out, "In an insecure and often violent world monastic communities were, or were intended to be, havens of security."[5] By practicing hospitality and creating havens of peace, monasteries thus indirectly began to affect the culture of the broader society.

Just like these early Irish monasteries, a key task of Ben Op communities will be extending the same kind of hospitality to their surrounding communities. Rather than doing this through guest houses, however, they will do it by offering third spaces. What is a third space? Urban planner and consultant Hazel Borys explains:

---

2. Hunter, *Celtic Way of Evangelism*, 42.
3. Bede, *History of the English Church and People*, 195.
4. Sheldrake, *Living between Worlds*, 38–39.
5. Fletcher, *Barbarian Conversion*, 91.

Building the Benedict Option

First place is our home, second place is where we work. Third places can range from a coffee house, a pub, or any place where the clientele is not really treated as a customer as much as a member of the community.[6]

As Sarah Joy Proppe points out, third places can play an integral part of the church showing hospitality to its neighbors:

The church has a significant role to play [in seeking] the flourishing of our neighborhood . . . [by] creating these third places . . . where people can gather, to serve the poor, the widow, the aliens in our land . . . The church has an opportunity to play a significant role in creating third places that really speak to the welcomeness [sic] *to strangers.*[7]

According to recent research by the American Enterprise Institute, "The most impactful third places are spaces of private consumption, such as cafes and restaurants, and not [as is often thought] public facilities like community centers and libraries."[8] Therefore, one potential way a Ben Op community will express hospitality to its broader community and help build social infrastructure will be creating and running a neighborhood coffee shop.

---

6. Jacobsen and Proppe, "Third Places and the Church," interview with Hazel Borys.

7. Jacobsen and Proppe, "Third Places and the Church."

8. Abrams, "What Are the Real Third Places?," §2.

The Coffee Shop

Ebenezer's is an example of one church seeking to express hospitality to its community through a third space. Another is Corner Church in the Twin Cities region of Minnesota. Pastor Scott Woller and a committed team of locals who had a passion for their community came up with the idea of combining a church with a coffee shop. They felt it was a natural way to both connect with neighbors and build relationships within walking distance of where they lived and worshiped. Through the church's coffee shop, Corner Coffee, they've been able to get to know regular neighborhood customers while bringing the gospel to their community in a way that feels authentic.

While a coffee shop may seem an obvious choice for any Ben Op community, Woller offers words of caution:

> *A coffee shop is a for-profit business. . . . The reality of a coffee shop is that it has three elements that any wise business man or woman would never run into: (1) You have to pay a lot for the space it's in, (2) it's labor intensive and people are more expensive than ever, and therefore (3) it's low margin. Making bucket loads of money is not going to be easy, or even possible. . . . At the beginning we had to supplement everything.*[9]

One of the primary expenses associated with running a coffee shop will be payroll. While using volunteers may be one way to keep costs down, it can present challenges in terms of quality of service. Another potential pitfall is that most churches just don't know how to run a business. A simple answer is to find someone within your church with business experience and get them excited about the idea, or find someone from outside your church who wants to start their own business and partner with them. Just make sure they share your same basic values. One of the biggest pitfalls is having what one practitioner cautions is a "field of dreams scenario": the belief that if you build a coffee house, people will automatically come.[10]

---

9. Jacobsen and Proppe, "Third Places and the Church," interview with Scott Woller.

10. These suggestions and cautions come from a conversation with Matt

The reality is that to run a coffee shop well requires a tremendous amount of time and effort. Nevertheless, despite the hurdles, many churches are successfully creating coffee shops that are a tangible expression of hospitality and provide a gathering space for their neighborhoods. Therefore, a coffee shop will be an integral part of many Ben Op communities. If a coffee shop appears too daunting however, there is another type of third space with potentially fewer hurdles that we'll examine next.

Busby, senior associate at Mission Chattanooga.

Chapter 7

The Coworking Space
Fostering Collaboration, Strengthening the Church

One should never direct people towards happiness, because happiness too is an idol of the marketplace. One should direct them towards mutual affection. A beast gnawing at its prey can be happy too, but only human beings can feel affection for each other, and this is the highest achievement they can aspire to.

—ALEKSANDR SOLZHENITSYN, *CANCER WARD*

Cultural Shift

From almost the inception of the United States, the White Protestant church has occupied a dominant position in North American culture. To be a Christian and a faithful churchgoer gave one a social cachet and allowed church leaders stridently to proclaim the existence of a "moral majority." But a tectonic cultural shift has occurred under the feet of American Christians, so quickly that many are still unaware of the radically new environment they now face. As Aaron Renn points out:

Building the Benedict Option

> *Christians now are a moral minority, even if a sizable one. One of the implications is that now being a minority group Christians need to start thinking and acting like a minority group. Dominant majority groups seldom have to worry too much about how to institutionally sustain their community because the mainstream institutions of society are designed in a manner that is consistent with and even reinforces, their values (e.g., boy scouts, elite colleges, public schools, fair play, etc.) . . . Up through the 1950's the major institutions of American society were linked culturally and institutionally with elite American Protestantism. . . . The experience of minority groups is generally very different. They have to focus on self-consciously sustaining their culture and community life as well, including creating their own bespoke institutions to serve their community. . . . They also have to specifically steward their own community well-being and mobilize to advocate on its behalf. We see this most clearly in the case of black Americans.*[1]

The Irish monks who set about re-evangelizing and re-civilizing Western Europe knew that they were a minority group, surrounded by a largely hostile, or at best, indifferent culture. Their approach of creating monastic settlements recognized that in order to successfully penetrate and transform the surrounding pagan culture, they first had to create a structure that would nourish, support, and protect an alternative Christian culture; they had to self-consciously sustain their own cultural and community life. And much of the appeal of their communities, and therefore their gospel, was that they were islands of peace, hospitality, and order in a sea of violence, social disorder, and anomie. And, as stated earlier, they didn't divide the world between secular and sacred, but incorporated space for workshops as well as for worship.

One of the chief ways the church of the twenty-first century can nourish and support a minority culture in an increasingly post-Christian landscape is to create coworking spaces specifically for other Christian organizations. Such a coworking space would help to self-consciously sustain and nourish an alternative Christian

---

1. Renn, "In Praise of the Private Good."

culture in a variety of ways, and thus should be an integral component of any Ben Op community. By creating a coworking space for local ministries and other faith-based organizations, and offering that space on a sliding scale, such a monastic settlement would:

1. Further the mission of Christian organizations by allowing them to put more of their money toward their respective missions, thus helping advance God's purposes in the broader community
2. Provide an income stream for the host church through rental income
3. Foster collaboration among Christian organizations

There couldn't be a better time to create a coworking space. More people are teleworking than ever before, and the trend doesn't look to be receding. Since the pandemic in 2020, a survey contracted by a county in the Washington, DC, area found that 74 percent of respondents had begun or increased teleworking.[2] According to data from the U.S. Census Bureau, nationally more than a third of families in 2021 reported they were working more frequently from home as a result of the pandemic.[3] In addition, the current housing crisis isn't just affecting homebuyers and renters, it's affecting ministries as well. Many Christian churches and organizations struggle to find affordable office space. Ben Op communities can take advantage of these trends by providing a coworking space at an affordable, below-market rent (along with other third spaces like a coffee shop).

Friendship, Clubs, and Intellectual Ferment

Another potential outcome of creating such a space is the possible creativity and intellectual ferment that can result from the interplay of creative minds in regular contact: iron really does sharpen iron under the right circumstances. What do I mean? Despite the myth of the lone genius producing a flood of intellectual output,

2. National Community Survey, "Loudoun County, VA."
3. Marshall et al., "Those Who Switched to Telework."

the evidence often points to something else: small groups of leaders developing friendships over shared conversation and often meals, leading to an intellectual ferment resulting in tremendous artistic output. As Jacques Barzun points out, the *sine qua non* for cultural flourishing is not "prosperity, or wise government support, or a spell of peace and quiet. . . . The first requisite is surely the clustering of eager minds in one place."[4]

History is replete with such groups, or clubs, and the intellectual ferment they produced was truly remarkable. As Philip and Carol Zaleski point out, such groups include:

> The 17th century Friday Street Club at the Mermaid Tavern in Cheapside, with its boisterous Elizabethan roster of Ben Johnson, John Donne, and Francis Beaumont; the early 18th century Scriblerus Club, a Tory group led by Alexander Pope, Jonathan Swift, John Arbuthnot . . .; and, later in the 18th century, Samuel Johnson's dinner-and-discussion circle, generically entitled "The Club," with Joshua Reynolds, Oliver Goldsmith, [and] Edmund Burke, (Adam Smith, and Edward Gibbon)."[5]

The supreme example for Christians of such a group is the Inklings: the group of friends that included J. R. R. Tolkien, C. S. Lewis, Charles Williams, and Owen Barfield.[6] According to Philip and Carol Zaleski:

> The [Inklings] . . . altered in large or small measure, the course of imaginative literature, Christian theology and philosophy, comparative mythology, and the scholarly

---

4. Barzun, *From Dawn to Decadence*, 67.
5. Zaleski and Zaleski, *Fellowship*, 27.
6. Many scholars assert that the members of the Inklings had little if any influence on one another. The Inklings themselves repeated this assertion, claiming to be, in the words of Robert E. Havard, little more than "simply a group of C. S. Lewis' wide circle of friends who lived near enough to him to meet regularly together." Diana Pavlac Glyer, in her book *The Company They Keep*, pushes back against this notion, however, asserting that the members did in fact have an influence on each other's writings. Pavlac Glyer, *Company They Keep*, xvi–xvii.

The Coworking Space

study of the Beowulf author, of Dante, Spenser, Milton, courtly love, fairy tale and epic.[7]

By providing a coworking space that encourages the leaders and pastors in a region to work in close proximity with one another, one increases the likelihood that such relationships will have a catalytic effect, resulting in increased intellectual and spiritual output.

Characteristics of an Effective Coworking Site

For the variety of reasons stated above, therefore, consider including in any proposed Ben Op community a coworking space. Build enough offices to house church staff and then build additional office space to rent on a sliding scale to other Christian ministries, organizations, and churches. Consider creating a joint coffee shop/coworking space.

When building such a space keep in mind the following suggestions:

1. Create a courtyard feel by providing a central coworking area, or hub

---

7. Zaleski and Zaleski, *Fellowship*, 4.

2. Provide individual offices opening off of the central coworking area
3. Offer high speed wifi and wired connections
4. Provide plenty of outlets
5. Create a neighborhood feel with different areas (i.e., areas with "library rules" and areas where people can be noisier)
6. Provide plenty of natural light[8]

The Importance of Networks

This leads to another intriguing possibility presented by such monastic settlements and their potential for fostering productive relationships between leaders. For hundreds of years, many people held that change was brought about primarily by special men and women. This was a view of history popularized by the nineteenth-century Scottish historian Thomas Carlyle. As Carlyle put it, "In all epochs of the world's history, we shall find the great man to have been the indispensable savior of his epoch." Among these great men, Carlyle included figures such as Moses, Mohammed, Alexander the Great, Julius Caesar, Plato, Aristotle, da Vinci, and Michelangelo. As sociologist James Davison Hunter points out in his book *To Change the World*:

> For Carlyle, heroes shaped history through the vision of their leadership, the power of their intellect, the beauty and delight of their aesthetic, and, animating it all, a certain inspiration from above. When the world's need is most acute, great leaders rise to the occasion and provide the courage and vision to address that need.

The only problem is that this perspective is wrong. A professor at the University of Virginia, Hunter has spent considerable time researching how societies change. And what he has found is that the key actor in history is not individual genius, but rather networks and the new institutions that are created out of such

8. Johnson, "10 Tips for Designing Your Coworking Space."

networks. While Hunter does concede that there often exists one person in a network who provides crucial leadership, it is the network of relationships within which this person functions that is crucial for true societal change.[9]

A clear example of the integral role such networks play in societal change can be found in the British abolition movement of the early nineteenth century. William Wilberforce was the British Parliamentarian most noted for spearheading the movement. But crucial to Wilberforce's success was what has come to be known as the Clapham Circle. This was a network of friends and associates consisting of over two dozen leaders from the highest echelons of business, church, literary life, government, and politics who were united in their opposition to the slave trade. As Hunter points out:

> In and through this network, they created numerous voluntary organizations, established strategic alliances, and made maximum use of the public media of the day—sermons, lectures, pamphlets, and newspapers.[10]

And such networks don't have to be that large to effect genuine change in a culture. According to Boleslaw Szymanski of the Rensselaer Polytechnic Institute, a committed minority of just under 10 percent can convert almost everyone to its way of thinking and cause the broader society to change its collective mind.[11] So, while remarkable individuals are important for societal change, even more important are networks of people unified by common goals and values, and the institutions they build.

This dynamic was an important part of the growth and eventual triumph of Christianity. The rise of large churches in key cities such as Rome, Alexandria, and Antioch, as well as the catechetical schools they founded, created the intellectual conditions for developing new leaders for the church who were conversant in pagan culture. The relationships these leaders developed with

---

9. Hunter, *To Change the World*, 38.
10. Hunter, *To Change the World*, 73.
11. Szymanski et al., "Social Consensus through the Influence."

one another then helped to influence the broader culture while advancing the interests of the Christian movement.

Another example of this dynamic at work, one that is more relevant to our purposes, is the Irish monastic movement itself. As Richard Fletcher points out:

> *The 6th century saw the foundation of a number of communities which were to achieve great renown in the history of Irish spirituality and learning—Bangor, Clonard, Clonfert, Conmacnois, Durrow, Kildare, Monasterboice, to name but a few. A feature of special significance for us is the appearance of monastic confederations spread over a wide area, chains of houses which owed their existence to a single founder and followed the rule drawn up by him.*[12]

These networks of monasteries working together were able to have a greater influence over a broader area than individual monasteries could ever have had. Therefore, they were crucial for the initial Christianization of Ireland, and the eventual re-evangelization of Western Europe. If a similar network of modern settlements could ever arise, united in a broad collaborative effort, who knows what type of cultural impact they could have? The idea is certainly intriguing, however implausible it may seem at the moment.

---

12. Fletcher, *Barbarian Conversion*, 92.

Chapter 8

The Christian Education Building
Restoring the Foundation

We may say also that in the whole history of man there is no education of a human soul unless the divine animates it. Otherwise it is mere training, fit for a dog, or habituation, fit for a machine, or political indoctrination, fit for no creature that has ever breathed upon earth.

—ANTHONY ESOLEN, *OUT OF THE ASHES*

Youth, Education, and Cultural Amnesia

A 2011 survey of Americans found that:
> only 30 percent knew that the Constitution is the supreme law of the land; 43 percent did not know that the first 10 amendments constitute the Bill of Rights; and two-thirds could not identify America's economic system as capitalistic or market-based.[1]

Another survey, by the American Council of Trustees and Alumni, found that:

---

1. Soifer, "Americans Are Dangerously Ignorant," §2.

Building the Benedict Option

More Americans could identify Michael Jackson as the composer of "Beat It" and "Billie Jean" than could identify the Bill of Rights as a body of amendments to the U.S. Constitution, more than a third did not know the century in which the American Revolution took place, and half of the respondents believed the Civil War, the Emancipation Proclamation or the War of 1812, were before the American Revolution.[2]

Increasingly, young people today know far more about pop culture than they do about their own cultural inheritance and history. Unfortunately, our system of higher education is doing little to address the problem. The Intercollegiate Studies Institute's 2007 survey found that graduating seniors at prestigious colleges and universities knew less American history than incoming freshmen did.[3] And according to Benjamin Schmidt of Northeastern University:

> *The number of bachelor's degrees granted in history declined from 34,642 in 2008 to 24,266 in 2017. . . . History departments are cutting courses and curtailing hires because of falling enrollments. The University of Wisconsin*

2. Boot, "Americans' Ignorance of History," §3.
3. Rozenman, "Like David McCullough, Americans' Ignorance," §10.

The Christian Education Building

at Stevens Point may even abolish its entire history department. History education in schools is so poor that students often enter college ignorant of the past—and leave just as unenlightened.[4]

And as distinguished historian David McCullough points out, "eighty percent of our colleges don't require history courses."[5]

Why is this growing historic amnesia a problem? Wilfred McClay explains:

> [The cultivation of history] is essential to the perpetuation of civilized life. History is to social identity what memory is to individual identity. Without the points of reference provided by historical consciousness, we soon forget who and what we are, and we perish. . . . A culture without memory will hardly be a culture at all.[6]

To read current surveys of young people's lack of historic knowledge is to see a people fast losing an understanding of their past, their culture, and the hard-won learning from literally thousands of years of civilization. Because of our material abundance and the ability to access almost unlimited information at the touch of a button, we fail to realize that it is in fact possible for us to forget. One is reminded of Neil Postman's words concerning Aldous Huxley's *Brave New World*:

> What Huxley feared was that there would be no reason to ban a book, for there would be no one who wanted to read one . . . [he] feared those who would give us so much that we would be reduced to passivity and egoism . . . [and, he] feared the truth would be drowned in a sea of irrelevance.[7]

One can see Postman's words as nothing other than eerily prescient.

When the Irish monks fanned out over Western Europe in the fading twilight of the Roman Empire they faced a situation not

---

4. Boot, "Americans' Ignorance of History" §2.
5. Rozenman, "Like David McCullough, Americans' Ignorance," §5.
6. McClay, "History as a Way of Knowing," §6, 8.
7. Postman, *Amusing Ourselves to Death*, vii.

unlike our own. With the disintegration of the empire in the West, knowledge began to be lost. Such knowledge included the secret of making Roman concrete and the ability to quarry and shape stone to the level of past Roman engineers. As serious as this loss of engineering knowledge was, however, far greater was the possibility that Western Europe might lose its Greco-Roman cultural and intellectual inheritance. As Thomas Cahill points out, with the increasing disintegration of the Roman Empire in the West, by AD 500 "all the great continental libraries had vanished: even memory of them had been erased from the minds of those who lived in the emerging feudal societies of medieval Europe."[8]

The Irish monks were ideally suited for the great task that lay ahead of them. Learning had always been central to the life of the Irish monasteries. Accordingly, as well as containing housing and workshops, Irish monastic settlements often included schools for educating both monks and laity, and scriptoria for the copying and preservation of manuscripts. As a result, one of the most important cultural contributions made by the Irish monastic movement was the preservation of classical learning at a time when it was quickly being lost throughout Western Europe. As John Finney points out, wherever they went, the Irish monks:

> *Began to educate. Initially, through preaching and verbal communication, and later through schools and the wider introduction of reading and writing, people were taught the faith. . . . Soon children began to be taught in monasteries and convents. At first, they were the offspring of royalty and the nobility. . . . However, even in the early days, [the monk's program of education] was not confined to the aristocracy. Promising boys and girls would be taken into the monastery at an early age and educated.*[9]

And as Cahill points out:

> *Latin Literature would almost surely have been lost without the Irish, and illiterate Europe would hardly have developed its great national literatures without the example*

---

8. Cahill, *How the Irish Saved Civilization*, 183.
9. Finney, *Recovering the Past*, 72.

of the Irish, the first vernacular literature to be written down. Beyond that, there would have perished in the west not only literacy, but all the habits of mind that encourage thought.[10]

As a result of their focus on education and the preservation of learning, Ireland experienced a cultural renaissance in learning at the exact moment at which learning in Western Europe was beginning to be lost. The result was monastic "university towns" that began to attract scholars from England, Western Europe, and as far away as Constantinople. Aldhelm, abbot of Malmesbury, wrote in AD 675 of boats full of Englishmen traveling to Ireland to study. Or as T. M. Charles-Edwards puts it:

> *For much of the seventh century, . . . Ireland was not just a pimple upon the outer skin of the known world, as the Irishman Cummian described his native island . . . . it was the resort of students anxious for advancement in the Christian Latin learning common to Western Europe, and also of young monks eager to gain knowledge of the monastic training which had produced Columbanus and Aidan.*[11]

One of the greatest contributions the Irish made to the revival of learning in Europe was their influence on the Carolingian king Carolus Magnus, better known as Charlemagne.

> *Charlemagne presided over medieval Europe's first Renaissance, a short-lived flowering that barely outlasted his reign. His enduring influence [however] lay in the gradual revival of literacy . . . Without the previous and continuing influx of Irish codices, the Carolingian Renaissance would have been impossible.*[12]

Several learned Irish monks served at the Frankish court and instructed the emperor in a variety of disciplines, including

---

10. Cahill, *How the Irish Saved Civilization*, 193–94.
11. Edwards, *Early Christian Ireland*, 9.
12. Edwards, *Early Christian Ireland*, 207.

astronomy, geography, and statecraft, thus helping ensure that the flickering light of learning in the West would not be extinguished.

In a similar way, Ben Op communities will help to preserve learning while educating the next generation by providing space for Christian schools. This may perhaps be the most important contribution it makes to the long term health of its community. Success in our modern culture is largely dependent on access to a good education, and providing this to its community is one of the ways the church can tangibly reflect Christ's love.

While education is important for the broader society, however, education rooted in a Judeo-Christian worldview is even more important for the church if it is to survive in the years ahead. If one considers such talk to be febrile, they are blissfully unaware of the massive cultural shift taking place beneath their feet.

According to current data, a mass exodus from the church is taking place, particularly among the young. According to the Pew Foundation:

> *Since the 1990s, large numbers of Americans have left Christianity to join the growing ranks of U.S. adults who describe their religious identity as atheist, agnostic or "nothing in particular." This accelerating trend is reshaping*

the U.S. religious landscape ... [In 2020], people who are religiously unaffiliated, sometimes called religious "nones," accounted for 30% of the U.S. population. Projections show Christians of all ages shrinking from 64% to between a little more than half (54%) and just above one-third (35%) of all Americans by 2070. Over that same period, "nones" would rise from the current 30% to somewhere between 34% and 52% of the U.S. population.[13]

And the Barna Group reports that:

In 2000, 45 percent of all those sampled qualified as practicing Christians. That share has consistently declined over the last 19 years. As of early 2020, just one in four Americans (25%) qualified as a practicing Christian. In essence, the share of practicing Christians has nearly dropped in half since 2000.[14]

According to recent research from the American Enterprise Institute, one of the chief factors driving this decline in religiosity is the public school system. Lyman Stone explains:

First, explicitly sectarian governance, such as having a state religion, tends to reduce religiosity, because it reduces the competitiveness and diversity of the religious marketplace. Second, expansions in government service provision and especially increasingly secularized government control of education significantly drive secularization and can account for virtually the entire increase in secularization around the developed world.[15]

If Stone is correct, one of the primary reasons for the decline in religiosity among the young is because the church handed over its responsibility to educate its youth to the State. If we are to reverse the current trend, churches must begin to get serious about supporting private schools that will provide students with a rigorous education grounded in the Judeo-Christian tradition. Such schools, while highlighting other cultures, are also not afraid

13. Pew Research Center, "Modeling the Future of Religion," §1, 4.
14. Barna, "Year in Review," §9.
15. Stone, "Promise and Peril," 1.

to draw from the deep and rich cultural inheritance of the West. One encouraging sign in this regard has been the rise over the past several decades of the classical education movement.

Such an investment in education will also be an indication that the church, after years of emphasizing a youth group culture that all too often has been a mile wide and an inch deep, is getting serious about catechizing its young people. It is finally recognizing that the one or two hours a week a young person spends in church are wholly incapable of shaping Christian disciples in the face of an increasingly hostile culture.

Therefore, any group seeking to develop a Ben Op should consider constructing a Christian education building to house its Sunday school and adult education classrooms. It should then make it available for use by a local Christian school during the week. This would mean constructing the building with two or three additional offices for use by school staff, and including ample storage for school supplies. By offering such space on a sliding scale (i.e., according to the school's resources), a Ben Op community will be making one of its most important contributions to its community, and to the future of the church, by investing in the young of today.

James Davison Hunter, again in *To Change the World*, points out that the creation of schools was crucial to the success of the early church. As he puts it:

> *Education was exceptionally important. . . . Much of the spiritual and cultural creativity of the church resided in the establishment and transformation of the schools of that time. . . . The schools not only were functional in forming potential leaders in the church. They were also the primary settings in which intellectual vitality was generated and influence in the culture was exerted.*[16]

The early church understood the importance of founding networks of schools that grounded their education in a Judeo-Christian worldview. Hunter's words are a timely reminder to

---

16. Hunter, *To Change the World*, 51–52.

the contemporary church, of the importance of doing the same thing today.

Chapter 9

The Construction
Planting the Trees Your Grandchildren Will Sit Under

The buildings our predecessors constructed paid homage to history in their design, including elegant solutions to age-old problems posed by the cycles of weather and light, and they paid respect to the future in the sheer expectation that they would endure through the lifetimes of the people who built them. They therefore embodied a sense of chronological connectivity, one of the fundamental patterns of the universe: an understanding that time is a defining dimension of existence—particularly the existence of living things, such as human beings, who miraculously pass into life and then inevitably pass out of it.

—JAMES HOWARD KUNSTLER, *HOME FROM NOWHERE*

They Don't Make 'Em Like They Used To

"They don't make them the way they used to." This oft-heard phrase applies to nothing if not to much current construction.

The Construction

Historically in the United States, it was not unusual for a family to build a dwelling with the belief that it would be passed down to future generations who would be rooted in that community for decades to come. We built for permanence. In contrast, as Ann Sussman points out, "the average stay of an American in their house is 13 years."[1] Very little sense of permanence remains in modern American society. This is reflected in another oft-heard phrase, "He'll go far." A person will be a success to the degree to which they leave the community in which they grew up. And so, while past generations were born, raised, and settled in a local community, today, families regularly wind up scattered to the four winds (or two coasts). One is expected to pursue his or her career at the expense of family and of being rooted in a local community.

This rootlessness is reflected in much modern construction. It's just not built to last, and why should it be? Many families will most likely move within a few brief years. And in most cases, there is certainly no thought that the children will inherit the house (and certainly not share it with parents). As developer Aaron Lubeck puts it:

---

1. Sussman and Hollander, *Cognitive Architecture*, 2.

Building the Benedict Option

> *There's a concept we were playing with a couple of years ago called the housing horizon. It would be defined as, "What is the longest time in years out, you can extrapolate the effects, the cost and benefits of the decisions you're making today."... Probably 100–150 years ago if you were building a house you were likely to build it with your own hands, you were likely to build it as your family's forever home. That was your horizon. It [went] beyond your lifetime into your children's lifetime. As we got into industrial building in the 1910's, 1920's somebody else might have built it for you, but it was still likely to be a family home, or you were likely to see it that way. Your horizon was at least 20, 30 maybe even 50 years. Then we got into production building where it probably compressed to 20, we became more mobile, [and] you'd probably move to Florida. The housing horizon probably hit its all-time low in 2006 where everybody was flipping homes... [It] became 24 months, because that was the minimum you could stay in your house and sell it tax free.*[2]

Having such a short housing horizon has a direct and deleterious effect on quality, because as Lubeck explains:

> *The way this extrapolates is when you're making a decision to whether you put in laminates or hard surface countertops or something like that, it's only a matter of "Can we sell this house in two years and move on. Does it make a difference with this, and if it doesn't, don't do it."*[3]

Such an approach has led to what has somewhat euphemistically been called "value engineering." This is ostensibly to save money, but it can lead to buildings constructed of material akin to Styrofoam with a faux brick covering.[4] One Anglican priest I know was hired by a church that had just moved into its newly constructed building. Being told that the foreman was coming by to place the "cornerstone" of the new building, he stared in

---

2. Marsh, "Incrementalism."
3. Marsh, "Incrementalism."
4. Known as an "Exterior Insulation Finishing System" (EIFS), or "Exterior Wall Insulation System" (EWI).

disbelief as the man took a pocket knife out of his pocket, proceeded to cut a chunk out of the side of the church, and then glued the "cornerstone" in place.

Accompanying this drop in quality construction has been a corresponding drop in the skills required to build well: we are literally losing the construction skills and knowledge our forefathers possessed. Christian developer John Marsh explains:

> We say the builders of today are really private equity guys, not master builders. Our cities are built today largely by people who do not have [fundamental carpentry] skills. Our communities, suburbia, are created by people who aren't craft people, who really don't have those skills which have been lost.

If, however, being the *imago Dei* means we are called to be God's vice-regents and follow him in the process of creation, of building, we must strive to create like God. We need to create things we can declare "good." We must flatly reject our culture's focus on the temporary, cheap, and rootless, and instead insist on building with excellence, building that which has permanence, building well. We need to build with a housing horizon that encompasses generations to come. We should plant the trees under which our grandchildren will sit. To do otherwise is to give into the spirit of our age and insult the God in whose image we are created. Dorothy Sayers expresses this feeling well in her 1942 essay "Why Work?":

> *The church's approach to an intelligent carpenter is usually confined to exhorting him not to be drunk and disorderly in his leisure hours, and to come to church on Sundays. What the church should be telling him is this: that the very first demand that his religion makes upon him is that he should make good tables. Church by all means, and decent forms of amusement, certainly—but what use is all that if in the very center of his life and occupation he is insulting God with bad carpentry? No crooked table legs or ill-fitting drawers ever came out of the carpenter's shop at Nazareth. Nor, if they did, could anyone believe that they were made by the same hand that made Heaven and earth.*[5]

Again, *how* we build is just as important as *what* we build. Therefore, as we seek to build Ben Op communities, we should seek to build them with quality material, an appreciation for beauty, and an attention to detail. And we should build them in such a way that they'll be around for years to come.

Perhaps the greatest hurdle to building well, however, is simply the cost. It's one reason we build "stick built" houses today with boards and drywall instead of solid masonry. One thing is certain: anyone seeking to build today will be faced with the competing claims of quality versus affordability and, most likely, will have to attempt to find a balance between the two. One possible way around this dilemma is to build in stages, with each component of the settlement helping to generate the income required to build the next (more on this later). But doing so will require taking the long view, and resisting our culture's tendency toward the immediate.

---

5. Sayers, "Why Work?," 114.

The Construction

Location, Location, Location

Talk to any realtor about what to look for when house shopping, and you'll likely be met with the oft-heard mantra "Location, location, location." This is equally important when considering the location of a Ben Op community. Therefore, it's helpful to keep in mind the example of the Irish monastic settlements. According to Richard Fletcher, "The Celtic monasteries organized to penetrate the pagan world and to extend the church," and therefore, "the Celtic Christians typically built their monasteries in locations accessible to the traffic of the time, such as proximity to settlements, on hilltops, or on islands near established sea-lanes."[6] The implication for us today is to look for enough land to provide space for such a development, while still being close enough to urban centers of influence.

Again, as with construction, this will involve a balancing act between price savings and land that is "strategically" located (and thus more expensive). Faith communities typically look for cheap land which tends to be in the suburbs or the far edge of town. While this is understandable, it merely reinforces the increasing marginalization of the church. Out of sight really is out of mind. Instead, when looking for land for your Ben Op community, consider looking for real estate closer to the center of town or, if in suburbia, in a more prominent location. By doing so, you will be making a public statement that the church is an integral part of the local culture. Of course, with real estate being as high as it is, doing so will require thinking outside the box. For instance, this might mean instead of building new construction on the edge of town, looking to purchase an older church building near the center of town and repurposing it. With the decline of the mainline denominations, this is not as unlikely as it once was. In addition, such historic church buildings are often built to a degree of quality (not to mention beauty) not usually found in much new construction. The point is, that if place really matters, then location does too.

---

6. Hunter, *Celtic Way of Evangelism*, 16.

One of the challenges pointed out earlier is that, because of modern urban planning, in many communities there remain very few actual city centers. Many of our cities and towns lack the architectural hierarchy that used both to reflect and reinforce a sense of social order and cohesion. Historically, the importance of institutions to the flourishing of a community was reflected both in their location (at the city center) and their design. Banks were built in such a way as to express solidity and strength, courts were built to reflect a grandeur and connection to the past, and churches were built to draw the gaze upward and remind citizens that they lived under the canopy of heaven. Today, in many communities, this has been replaced by a landscape of undifferentiated, anodyne suburbs. Lacking any real center they merely reinforce the isolation of modern society and foster the notion that the autonomous self and its desires are the center of life. There's no "strategic" real estate left for churches to buy.

It is precisely here that Ben Op communities hold out hope. In suburbs that lack a city center, they can become a hub around which to begin rebuilding a sense of shared community, shared culture. In doing so, they might help repair our social fabric while ensuring the church a central role in addressing our current ills.

Chapter 10

Charting a Course Forward

We all want progress. But progress means getting nearer to the place where you want to be. And if you have taken a wrong turning, then to go forward does not get you any nearer. If you are on the wrong road, progress means doing an about-turn and walking back to the right road; and in that case the man who turns back soonest is the most progressive man.

—C. S. LEWIS, THE CASE FOR CHRISTIANITY

Incremental Growth No More

Würzburg today is a university city of 130,000 located on either bank of the Main river. From St. Killian's Cathedral rising majestically over the city (the fourth largest Romanesque cathedral in Germany), to the Marienberg fortress perched on its hill overlooking the river, it offers "a vibrant atmosphere and endearing charm."[1] And yet it didn't start out this way. Settled by the Franks, Würzburg served as the seat of a Merovingian duke from about AD 650. It was Christianized in 686 by Irish missionaries Kilian, Kolonat, and Totnan, who created a monastic settlement to give

---

1. German National Tourist Board, "Würzberg," §1.

Building the Benedict Option

expression to their way of life and serve as a base of further evangelism to the surrounding area. It would be the first of multiple iterations of the settlement that, over the centuries, grew gradually from a small village of thatched houses, into a bustling city of stone buildings and all of the municipal infrastructure required to support modern life.

The culture we inhabit today is worlds away from that of Kilian, Kolonat, and Totnan. Probably the greatest difference is just the sheer complexity of modern life, with its byzantine array of rules and regulations governing every aspect of existence. This is particularly true in the area of development and land use. Gone are the days when a team of intrepid pioneering monks could construct a settlement of rude huts that would eventually grow organically and incrementally over time into a city. Such an approach would quite frankly be illegal. Today it's necessary to have a detailed plan ahead of time for what a settlement will look like, a road map for how you will take your vision and make it a reality. So, assuming your congregation has through much prayer, conversation, and community input developed a vision for a settlement, how do you then make it a reality?

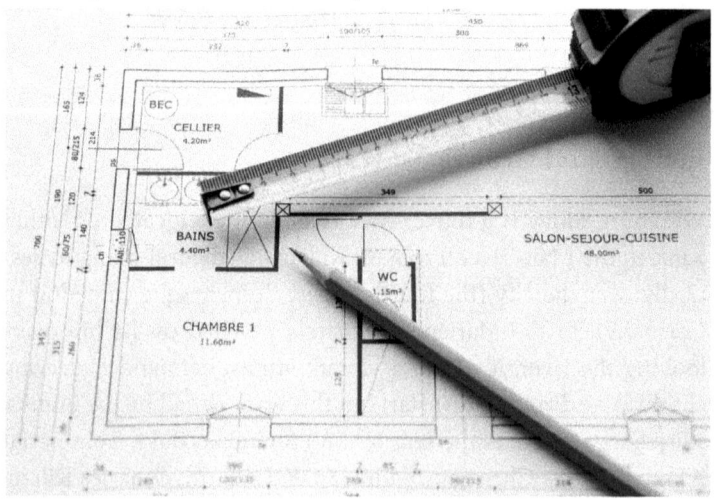

The Process

Step One: Architect

The first step is to find an architect who can help you further refine your vision and who will ultimately produce an architectural rendering that is faithful to your vision. One of the difficulties you'll face as you set out to build a Ben Op community is that most schools of architecture don't teach along New Urbanist principles or encourage traditional architecture. Notre Dame University (https://architecture.nd.edu) and the Classic Planning Institute (https://www.classicplanning.org/about) are two organizations that do. They may be able to point you to architects in your area who share similar values. Once you have a rough architectural rendering of your plan in hand, it's time to move to the next step: finding an engineer.

Step Two: Engineer

A real estate engineer will take a look at the architectural rendering provided by your architect and compare it to the zoning ordinance, the facilities and standards manual, and the codified ordinance (all of which determine how development is done in your municipality). They'll then highlight for you all the things you'll have to overcome in order to make your vision a reality. With this information in hand, you'll then need to find a good lawyer.

Step Three: Lawyer

A real estate development attorney will be able to help you with all aspects of subdivision and land development. They'll tell you what you might have to amend to comply with current law, or whether you can receive a waiver for certain aspects of your development. You'll then go back to your plan and revise it according to their input. Once this has been done, you'll have a fully fleshed out vision that's had an initial review by knowledgeable people and that you can take to a developer.

Step Four: Developer

A real estate developer is someone who specializes in the development or redevelopment of properties. They will take your project from start to finish and manage all of the various actors involved such as contractors, architects, etc.

One organization that can help orient you to the development process is the Incremental Development Alliance. IncDev offers day-long, intensive "Workshops" and "Bootcamps" to orient you to the development process from start to finish (https://www.incrementaldevelopment.org).

While this process no doubt seems overwhelming, the important thing to remember is that just like marriage (or parenting), if you wait to do it until you feel ready, you never will. Instead, like those intrepid monks years ago setting out into the wide world from the safety of their monastery, believe that God is big enough not only to guide you to where you need to go, but also to provide you with the resources to get there.

Chapter 11

Hurdles to Clear

It is literally against the law almost everywhere in the United States to build the kind of places that Americans themselves consider authentic and traditional. It's against the law to build places that human beings can feel good in, or afford to live in. It's against the law to build places that are worth caring about.

—JAMES HOWARD KUNSTLER, *HOME FROM NOWHERE*

Planned Communities, Utopias, and Other Pipe Dreams

In 1841, a small group of nineteenth-century luminaries, including Ralph Waldo Emerson and Nathaniel Hawthorne, founded an experimental community they called the Brook Farm Institute of Agriculture and Education. Established on two hundred acres in West Roxbury, Massachusetts, its stated purpose was to offer a life based on the principles of "plain living." Brook Farm was part of a movement that swept America in the 1840s that saw hundreds of planned, often utopian, communities founded. Such communities, in the words of Richard Francis:

Building the Benedict Option

> *Reflected large-scale political and social unease running through America. . . . The broad impulse behind [the communities] . . . was a reaction to the industrial revolution and the rise of cities, with their consequent social injustice, poverty, and environmental deterioration.*[1]

As well as intellectuals, Brook Farm attracted farmers, printers, shoemakers, and carpenters, and included a college preparatory course, primary school, and an infant school. It eventually grew to include 120 people.[2]

As Transcendentalists, the founders of Brook Farm asserted the fundamental inherent goodness of human nature. No less a resident than Emerson:

> *Announced the residence of the divine within the individual and the conviction about an "infinite" worthiness of human beings together with the belief that reform simply meant removing "impediments" to natural perfection.*[3]

Alas, the members of the community proved all too incapable of achieving their "natural perfection" and relational conflict ensued. As a result, members like Nathaniel Hawthorne began to drift away. After struggling on valiantly for a number of years, the community eventually dissolved, selling its land and buildings in 1849.

To propose the type of Ben Op developments that have been argued for in this work might seem to many to be merely just one more harebrained endeavor in the line of Brook Farm and the myriad other such utopian and short-lived communities founded in the nineteenth century (and more recently during the counter-cultural wave of the sixties). Or worse, it might be seen as modelling itself after fringe, cult-like groups like the Branch Davidians hunkering down in their heavily armed compounds to keep out a threatening modern world.

---

1. Francis, *Fruitlands*, 3.
2. National Park Service, "Utopias in America."
3. Requena Pelegri, "Nathaniel Hawthorne's Minority Report," 99.

But to argue such is to concede to our post-Christian culture's assertion that faith should only ever be a private matter and to ignore the long history of such endeavors in America that have worked: from the communities founded by the Puritans in New England to the numerous towns founded by Saxon Lutherans in Missouri in the early 1800s.[4] It is also to ignore the communities built by early twentieth-century urban planners along such lines: communities like Forest Hills Gardens in the borough of Queens in New York City. As Ross Chapin explains in his book *Pocket Neighborhoods*:

> Renowned landscape architect Frederick Law Olmstead Jr. and architect Grosvenor Atterbury led the charge to design a verdant pedestrian scale village of 900 homes, townhouses, and apartment buildings, with a commercial hub, a public school, and a community building for cultural and recreational activities. Included are house clusters and short, defined blocks with shared common greens. . . . More than 100 years later, their plan remains intact, a testament to their vision.[5]

Even in my own Anglican tradition, there have existed prominent voices arguing for just such an approach. One such is the early twentieth-century architect Ralph Adams Cram, who designed Princeton and most famously St. John the Divine Cathedral in New York City (and who even has his own feast day in the liturgical calendar!). Cram argued for what he called "walled towns," meaning not literal walled towns, but as he puts it:

> The phrase "Walled Towns" is symbolical only . . . . In addition to the groups of either men or women, living in a community life apart, and vowed to poverty, celibacy and obedience, there will be groups of natural families, mother and children, entering into a communal life, but not by any means "communistic" life, within those Walled Towns they will create for themselves, in the midst of the world but not of it, where the conditions of life will be determined after

---

4. Forster, *Zion on the Mississippi*.
5. Chapin, *Pocket Neighborhoods*, 35.

Building the Benedict Option

such sort as will make possible that real and wholesome and joyful and simple and reasonable living that has long been forbidden by the conditions of modern civilization.[6]

The church throughout its history has been at the very center of creating livable communities and settlements that foster human flourishing. The Irish monastic movement we've been examining is just one such effort. It is only in fairly recent times that we have forgotten this truth. If the idea of the church being at the center of designing such communities seems foreign to us, it is only because we have forgotten our own church (and American) history and acquiesced in our culture's quite recent claim that the church inhabits a religious sphere that is wholly separate from a "secular" sphere. But if the church is to regain its proper mission to the larger world, it must reclaim its inheritance of speaking to all of life. Otherwise, it will persist in inhabiting a private and very cramped world and continue to have little, if any, involvement in the process of renewing a culture that is deeply dysfunctional and broken.

But if one is not opposed to Ben Op communities on philosophical or theological grounds, there still often remain quite a few imposing hurdles to overcome in the realization of such a dream.

---

6. Crams, *Walled Towns*, 35–36.

The Problem with Zoning

If you set out to create a Ben Op in your own community, a hurdle you will almost immediately face will be what developer Ryan Terry calls, "regulatory contamination":

> The rules at city hall and the zoning code, building code don't allow good things to be built and the city doesn't change that. It doesn't matter what people want to do they're not allowed to do it.[7]

For instance, land for housing is often zoned "R1," which allows for only single-family homes and no other type of development. So a Ben Op that involves the type of "mixed-use" facilities proposed by this work will be illegal. And as author Daniel Parolek points out, even missing-middle housing is often not permitted on the smaller lot plans (e.g., six to twelve acres) suggested by this work.[8]

Thankfully, municipalities are beginning to recognize the benefit of mixed-use (i.e., traditional) development and responding by creating districts that give greater flexibility in terms of the range of building types that can be included. Sometimes referred to as "Planned Unit Developments" or " PUDs," such districts give developers almost unlimited freedom to do what they want: single family, multi-family, apartments, and commercial buildings are all permitted in the same location. Another option is to ask your local planning board for permission to create a "Traditional Neighborhood Development" (or "District"). Philip Bess explains how this is done:

> In order to make such projects a built reality, [you'll] typically have to change the zoning ordinances and the street design and parking regulations that effectively make traditional neighborhood design illegal. [This will involve] first proposing that a given area be designated as a "Traditional Neighborhood District" (TND) to be overlaid on whatever existing zoning map currently governs the use of the site;

---

7. Congress for the New Urbanism, "Incremental Development."
8. Parolek, "Q and A: Missing Middle."

and then by creating for the proposed TND four related legal devices: 1.) a master plan, 2.) a regulating plan, 3.) a simple, diagrammatic, visual form-based urban code, and 4.) a brief zoning ordinance written in more less plain English.[9]

So, while zoning is often the first hurdle to clear, thankfully there is a growing understanding on the part of local boards that developers need to be given greater flexibility in order to address the housing shortage present in so many communities.

Pushback from the Community

Although there is growing recognition of the benefits of traditional community development on the part of municipalities, you will very likely face pushback from any neighborhood you attempt to build in due to the apparent novelty of your proposed development. You may also very well meet with opposition (or at the least blank stares), when proposing it to your local board of supervisors. The answer is to hold the type of charrette discussed in chapter 4. Again, Philip Bess explains:

> *The primary means for . . . achieving public consensus . . . is a five-to-ten-day intensive design workshop known in New Urbanist circles as a "charrette." A charrette brings together in one place several groups of people important to any land development process. Among these groups is a design team comprising the many professionals needed to do traditional neighborhood design. This would include the urban designers, the architects, the landscape architects, the civil engineers, the transportation engineers, the hydrologists, the sanitation engineers, the fire and police department personnel responsible for emergency vehicle access, etc. Then there are the various project stakeholders: most obviously the developer, but also persons from the local planning department, bankers, various civic and business leaders, and so on. Last but not least, there is the general public. It is important to note that the assumption*

---

9. Bess, *Till We Have Built Jerusalem*, 124.

of a charrette is that everybody brings their own particular interests to it.... The charrette is a no-holds-barred public process with built in feedback mechanisms by means of which objectives are articulated, problems are identified and addressed, and community consensus is built around an end product that is visual, easy to understand.[10]

Local municipalities are often more amenable to a proposed development if it will provide amenities that will benefit the broader community. For instance, many northern towns lack indoor recreational facilities. You might therefore propose to build a church sanctuary that could double as a gymnasium during the week, and offer it for use by your local department of parks and recreation. Or, as part of your proposed Ben Op development, you might include space for a soccer field that could be used by the Christian school during school hours, and by your town in the afternoons and weekends. The point is, one way to overcome potential opposition is to show clearly how your proposed development will benefit the broader community.

---

10. Bess, *Till We Have Built Jerusalem*, 124–25.

Building the Benedict Option

Money, Money, Money

When contemplating a building campaign, many faith communities understandably look to their congregations to raise enough money to secure a loan from a bank. While your congregation may serve as the primary source for funding for your Ben Op community, you'll want to explore other sources as well. According to real estate developer Jim Heid, these may include:

> *High-net-worth (HNW) individuals:* An example is an "accredited investor," commonly described as having an investable net worth of at least $1 million and annual income in excess of $250,000. For HNW investors, this is generally an opportunistic business proposition, and returns need to be commensurate.
>
> *Family offices:* This is the term for operations that manage the legacy assets of wealthy families. Family offices seeking to define or enhance their missions while creating long-term returns may be better candidates for . . . pioneering projects if both mission and goals are aligned. But they will not invest on emotion only; there has to be a credible business proposition and assessment of risk.
>
> *Foundations:* In addition to grants, many foundations make program-related investments to further their missions, looking for return of capital and return on investment, albeit at a lower rate than conventional investors. Developers who can demonstrate that their projects satisfy both requirements may find foundations to be good sources of patient capital.
>
> *Grants, tax credits, etc.:* The equity sources in this catch-all category require no return and less investor management once the placement is consummated, but the up-front work is extensive in time and effort. However, mastering the intricacies of effective grant writing and reporting, historic tax credits, new market tax credits, conservation easements, etc., creates intellectual property that adds value to your enterprise and can be used in subsequent projects.[11]

---

11. Heid, "Lean Financing," 1–2.

One promising development has been the rise of "patient capital," sometimes known as "impact investment." These two terms refer to investors who aren't looking to make a fast buck. Instead, they want their money to make a lasting, positive change in a community, and they're willing to wait, sometimes even decades, to see a return on their investment. Family offices may be more willing to pursue such an approach and give money toward a project that stands to benefit the local community.

There is, of course, quite a bit of funding available from state, federal, and municipal sources to help build affordable housing. Such monies can be secured by a faith community as long as it commits to reserving a portion of its units for low-income individuals. While this may work well in some cases, there is a downside. Such money comes with strings attached and requires additional paperwork and reporting. This will constrain what you can and can't do with your property, and so churches considering this option should make sure to read the "fine print" before pursuing this course.

Build in Stages, or Mix and Match

The "template" proposed in this work for a Ben Op community is not meant to be rigid. In addition, it's not expected that a Ben Op will be built all at once. Instead, it will most likely be a long-term project that unfolds over many years, with earlier elements providing an income stream to help finance later elements.

Also, you don't have to build all of the elements included in the comprehensive model presented in this work. One of the strengths of the template is that each element by itself offers benefits. You can choose which elements you want to include according to the amount of land available and your particular context. If you don't want to build housing for instance, by providing amenities such as a coworking site, dog park, playground, and basketball courts, you can still become a hub around which your neighborhood can begin to build a sense of community, and thus do your part to help repair our fraying social fabric.

Even if new construction is not an option, if you are a church, there are many ways you can repurpose and adapt your current facility to better meet the needs of the community by incorporating some of the elements we've mentioned. Sara Joy Proppe and Edward Dunar offer several suggestions for how this can be done in their manual *Redemptive Placemaking: A Toolkit for Discerning Your Church's Mission in the Built Environment*:

1. Open your playground to the community during the week
2. Plant a community garden and invite neighborhood participation
3. Build a small outdoor patio or park for neighborhood gatherings
4. Host a local food truck on your parking lot and invite your neighbors
5. Provide places like benches in front of your church for people to rest[12]

The main idea is to begin to look for ways that you can use your facility and land to bless the community in which you're embedded: to "seek the peace of the city" to which God's called you.

---

12. Proppe and Dunar, *Redemptive Placemaking*.

Chapter 12

Mission Chattanooga

You can quote me on this. I think any city designer or neighborhood designer will tell you that one of the problems in our cities are these big empty church buildings that sit empty six days a week...

—ABBOT CHRIS SORENSEN

Saint Patrick, Dreams, and a Leap of Faith

The Irish were big believers in dreams. After all, the course of Saint Patrick's life was changed on two separate occasions by a dream. The first dream occurred while he was a slave. Having been captured by a band of Irish raiders as a boy of sixteen living in Roman Britain, he was taken back to Ireland where he tended sheep for six long years. Then one night while sleeping, he heard a voice declare, "See, your ship is ready." In obedience to the divine voice, he fled. Eventually after two hundred grueling miles he came upon a ship floating peacefully at anchor off the coast. It was his ticket back to the safety of family and friends in Britain. But it was not God's will that he should remain there. One night he had yet another dream. He describes it thus:

Building the Benedict Option

> *And there I saw in the night the vision of a man, whose name was Victoricus, coming as it were from Ireland, with countless letters. And he gave me one of them, and I read the opening words of the letter, which were, "The voice of the Irish"; and as I read the beginning of the letter I thought that at the same moment I heard their voice—they were those beside the Wood of Foclut, which is near the Western Sea . . . and thus did they cry out as with one mouth: "We ask you, boy, come and walk among us once more."*[1]

In obedience to the divine dream, Patrick returned to Ireland, now as someone gripped with the passion to reach his former captors with the good news of Jesus Christ. His labor would eventually help spark a spiritual awakening that would see Ireland transformed.

Today, God is raising up a new generation of intrepid followers, who aren't afraid to answer their own dreams and follow down the path blazed by Patrick and the Irish monastics so long ago. Two such individuals are Chris and Angela Sorensen.

In 2009, Angela Sorensen awoke from a deep sleep believing God had just spoken to her in a dream. At the time, she and her husband, Chris, were pastoring a church just north of New York City. Chris had studied anthropology and sociology at Nyack and been deeply influenced by George Hunter's book *The Celtic Way of Evangelism*. He came away from reading it believing that the way to reach the un-churched was to create a culture better than what the world was offering. As he puts it:

> *When people are hyper focused on this culture going to hell in a handbasket, the answer isn't to throw hand grenades at the culture but to offer something better than the culture. This means a focus not on whether it is Christian art, but whether it is high quality, beautiful art. This applies to businesses we've started as well. [It's] about creating culture, contributing to human flourishing, [and] providing opportunities for people.*[2]

1. Patrick, "Confession of St. Patrick," §28.

2. Unless otherwise noted, all quotes in this chapter are from interviews conducted by Ward Davis.

Another firm conviction Sorensen had was that the church needed to play a central role in the community. On a trip to England he had been struck by the many rural villages where a church formed the central point of the town. As he puts it:

> I noticed that the church was right in the center of each village. The whole village is built around the church. Then I came to find out, started asking about it, and discovered that not only was the church in the center of the village, the church was the center of education, it was a place of protection—people would run into it if marauders came, it was the place of commerce—because they would have days where people would show up with all their goods to trade. And I thought, man, this is it. The church is in the center of things.

After a brief visit to Chattanooga, they returned to their church in Connecticut and announced to the congregation that God was calling them to found a missional community in Tennessee. In response, seven members decided to join them. Like the teams of early Irish monks, they set off to a foreign place to recreate the community they had enjoyed at home.

Coffee, Art, Music, and Prayer: Southside

The church planting team was inspired by two Scripture passages. The first was God's charge to the Jews in Jeremiah 29:7: to "seek the peace and prosperity" of the city to which they'd been called. The other was John 1:14 in the Message translation: "The Word became flesh and blood and moved into the neighborhood." In obedience to these two passages they chose a neighborhood that at the time was written up in *U.S. News & World Report* as among the most dangerous neighborhoods in the US: Chattanooga's Southside. It was number eight on the list; over 40 percent of its residents had been victims of crime at some point, and 18 percent of violent crime.

Matt Busby is the senior associate at what became known as Mission Chattanooga (MC), and a member of the team since the early days. As he remarks, "The initial vision for the team was to plant in a downtown neighborhood and have a space that didn't sit empty 6 days a week but was a gift to the community throughout the week." Therefore, central to their whole approach was the creation of a third space that they hoped would become the central hub of activity for Southside.

After much prayer, the team rented an old warehouse in Southside and formulated a plan for what would become the CAMP House. With its acronym standing for "coffee, art, music and prayer," the CAMP House would eventually hold a coffee shop and other micro-businesses such as an art studio and thrift store. An intentionally neutral space, it would also serve as a venue for concerts, art shows, and other events during the week. On Sundays, it would serve as the meeting place for the church. Matt Busby explains:

> *The original vision was that the church wouldn't own any of the businesses inside, it would have all of these different micro-businesses during the week. But that could be converted into a church on Sundays. It's like planting in a school cafetorium but we owned the building. But everything about the building was oriented towards the community—towards the public facing aspect of who we were. So the CAMP House became a coffee shop and venue throughout the week and Mission Chattanooga was the church on Sunday. We were publicly a business, most people would walk into the CAMP House and not know we were owned by a church, we didn't hide that fact, if you looked around you could figure that out, but there wasn't Hillsong playing over the speakers when you walked in.*

Over the next five years, the small Christian community went from being out-of-towners whom people didn't know or trust, to becoming an indispensable instrument for human flourishing, and central to the revitalization of Southside.

The CAMP House, Southside
(images in this chapter are courtesy of Matt Busby).

Sarah Morgan is the president of the Benwood Foundation, a place-based, private foundation. They work with local nonprofits, businesses, and community and government leaders to support the "shared prosperity" of Chattanooga. Over the years she's seen the difference that MC has made. As she puts it:

> Frankly I was skeptical that a church would have an impact because they're only there on Wednesdays and Sundays. But they came in with a spirit of, "We love what we see in this neighborhood, we want to be a part of it, and we want to be a place where you want to come." So they changed the building to accommodate less forms of worship and it [really] did become an animator [for the neighborhood].

As a result, when after five years the owner of their building decided not to renew their lease, the Benwood Foundation and their city councilman approached them and offered to help them find another building. They were just too important to the ongoing renewal of downtown Chattanooga to lose. In 2014, they would eventually find a building for rent on MLK Boulevard on the west side of Chattanooga. As Busby puts it:

Building the Benedict Option

> The city would say that we played a role in the development of the Southside neighborhood, just our presence being there. So when we moved to MLK, part of the reason the Benwood Foundation went to the [owner of the building we were interested in] and said, "We know you want to redevelop this space, we want the CAMP House to be the anchor tenant on MLK" was because the city was looking at that area to redevelop.

History, Street Diets, and Business Associations: MLK Boulevard

Referred to as MLK Boulevard today, the neighborhood that Mission Chattanooga relocated to was once known as the "Big Nine."[3] Formerly the center of a nightclub district similar to Memphis's Beale Street, it featured a variety of African American–owned offices, retail shops, and entertainment venues.[4] After this period of prosperity, however, for a variety of reasons, the neighborhood fell on hard times. One of the biggest reasons for its decline was poor urban design. As Busby puts it:

> In the seventies, MLK went from being a two way road to four lanes going out of the city in one direction. Two blocks up was McCaulley Ave. coming into the city with four lanes. Whether you think it was intentional or not, this killed most of the Black businesses in that neighborhood.

The situation was only slightly improved in 2000, when the city belatedly took steps to fix the problem by changing the four one-way lanes to two lanes running both ways.

Being conscious of the way in which the MLK neighborhood had suffered historically either through neglect or overt racism, the congregation of MC saw themselves as partners who wanted to

---

3. In 1994, the community was listed on the National Register as "An area of great historical significance . . . the only cohesive area left that is historically associated with Chattanooga's African-American population" (*Nooga Today* Intern, "Visit Chattanooga's MLK District," §2).

4. *Nooga Today* Intern, "Visit Chattanooga's MLK District," §2.

come alongside and support those businesses and long-time residents who had courageously stuck it out through the hard times and were working diligently toward a brighter future.

The CAMP House, MLK

One of the first steps MC took moving into the neighborhood was to reestablish the CAMP House in their new location. This helped to create a gathering place for the community as well as increase economic activity. They also took another important step: They helped reestablish the MLK business association (calling it "The Big 9 Association"). This involved enlisting the support of local businesses to bring about a "road diet" by which the four lane road was reduced to three lanes (one lane in each direction with a turning lane). This helped to improve the overall "feel" of the street for both customers and neighbors, thus having a direct impact on local businesses. The end result was that when they moved five years later, having outgrown their space, seven new businesses had moved onto the street while the majority of the Black-owned businesses were still there.

Community Symposium, The CAMP House

Donut Holes, Partnership, and the Zombie Apocalypse: Onion Bottom 2020

In 2019, when MC began to realize they needed to find yet another building, because of their financial constraints and their commitment to the downtown area, the obvious choice was Onion Bottom. Chris Sorensen describes Onion Bottom in this way:

> [It's a] forgotten place, although it's five minutes from the most exclusive shopping in Chattanooga. It's not a thoroughfare, not even near a thoroughfare and it's not an area city developers were looking to develop. It's an area where you have supply warehouses. It looked like a zombie apocalypse had fallen on the area. It was an area that needed . . . redemption.

Matt Busby agrees:

> It's like a "donut hole in the center of town"; where the railroads come in and out: a bunch of warehouses with literally no infrastructure. So it's been very neglected. It's the center of the homeless community in the neighborhood.

Mission Chattanooga left MLK Boulevard because of space reasons. Therefore, when they moved to Onion Bottom, they wanted to make sure they had enough room for growth. God enabled them to work out a deal where they purchased twenty-five thousand square feet of a one-hundred-thousand-square-foot warehouse.

Onion Bottom

And because Onion Bottom's situation was more challenging than their previous locations, Sorensen realized they needed to shift more of their focus to mercy ministry. Therefore, instead of focusing on starting something brand new, they came into the neighborhood committed to partnering with the nonprofit organizations that were already there. One of the first steps they took, therefore, was to sit down with these same organizations and draw up a framework plan for the neighborhood. A framework plan is a plan of action to guide future growth and investment in a particular neighborhood; tangible evidence of MC's belief in the future of Onion Bottom and their continued commitment "to seek the peace and prosperity" of Chattanooga.

The Importance of Culture Making

It is a core premise of this work that the church needs to regain a sacramental theology that is concerned not only with saving people's souls, but also with a culture making that includes the built environment. Doing so is to regain our mission as image bearers of God called to complete the creational task given to Adam. This understanding is central to how the leaders of Mission Chattanooga see themselves and their mission. Matt Busby explains it this way:

> Where do you find value as a Christian? My upbringing and most Christians I know will say the Great Commission. That is true. But what they don't realize is that there was an original commission before that to go out and bring order to Creation. And it's through the life, death, and resurrection of Jesus that we're able to do what we do.

Chris Sorensen approaches culture making from two perspectives:

> The first is the cultural mandate in Genesis reflected in Revelation. God created a city. Eternity in city and glory of nations coming into city. Things that we make, God not only wants to spend eternity with us, but also with the things we made.
> The second part of culture making runs parallel. I don't think culture is ultimately ever reformed. I think it's replaced. [. . . We should] offer something better than [the prevailing] culture. The focus should not be on whether it is Christian art, but whether it is high quality, beautiful art. This applies to the businesses we've started. By creating culture [we're] contributing to human flourishing [and] providing opportunities for people.

But Mission Chattanooga understands something understood by the Irish monks, but often missed by contemporary evangelicals: Culture making involves the built environment. It needs to be embodied. Why? Busby explains:

> How do you reach your neighbor? What does it mean to love your neighbor today? I think those things have to be

answered in very embodied ways. It doesn't feel meaningful any more for people to just donate money. If people are going to be in community, they want to be in a community that has a value beyond themselves. At least I hope, that the desire to go to church, for my own spiritual fulfillment and my own spiritual needs, I really hope that vision of church is going to be on its way out. And so to look at the actions of your church and how your church lives its life in the community in a way that blesses its neighbors, to have real tangible things you can point to and people you can point to I think is really important and I think this model of church planting that takes the built environment seriously, all that's saying is that you take your neighborliness seriously, and how your neighbors move through the world and how you connect to them. Churches need to understand what it means to have an impact on their neighbors in an embodied way in order to love them. That's what Matthew 25 is all about.

Such an approach to "doing church" will, Busby believes, become even more important in the years ahead. As he puts it:

I just don't know that the model of church planting that we've had and the style of churches we've had over the past 100 years are going to survive. The reason people don't plant churches in cities is not because they're the big evil place where the Devil exists, but because you can't afford to. You can't afford real estate downtown. Part of the reason Chris planted this church the way that he did was because he approached it like a missionary. Mission-based businesses, that they do in foreign countries. It's not only a way into the country, that provides for them financially, it's a way into the community period. You're not going to make relationships otherwise. I think both those realities are increasingly important in a post-Christian America. Number one, is being out in the community to love your neighbor in a real tangible way, but also it creates a way for you to be in places you couldn't be in otherwise, just from a financial perspective.

All Politics Is Local

Former Speaker of the House Tip O'Neil was famous for opining that "all politics is local." Evangelicals seem to have forgotten this truth. While they have increasingly focused on national politics, they have tended to overlook the importance of local politics. As a result, many pastors today have little understanding of their municipal government. Nor do they appreciate the impact that building good relationships with municipal officials can have on their church's reputation and influence in the community.

The CAMP House, Onion Bottom

The leaders of MC were no different when they first moved to Chattanooga. Over time, however, they've grown to appreciate the importance of developing a close relationship with local officials. This has benefited the mission in a variety of ways. For instance, when the owner of their building in Southside decided not to renew their lease, their local city official became their *de facto* real estate agent and helped them secure a new building at MLK. Their relationship was so good, in fact, that Chris Sorensen is convinced that, had they gotten into financial trouble along the way, the city would have bailed them out.

The CAMP House, Onion Bottom

It must be said that in the Black community, officials have traditionally seen the church as a key institution and an integral part of the community's fabric. This is particularly true in an urban context. For example, if there is a community tragedy, any press conference that is held will likely be in one of the community's Black churches. The situation is quite different when it comes to the White church. This is particularly true in suburbia where local officials and neighbors often see churches as a liability, especially when they are contemplating new construction. Concerns about the church's impact on available parking or traffic flow often lead to an adversarial relationship. Churches by and large are not seen as adding much value to the community or as being concerned with the practical problems often faced by city officials and neighborhoods. It doesn't have to be this way, however. Busby explains:

> I think churches in general need to become better about thinking about their impact on a city in ways the city cares about. If you care about the shalom of your city, there's a very beautiful central Venn diagram, a big circle in the middle, that actually cares about a lot of the same things that your city councilman cares about. If you can talk about your church having a social impact that's beyond, you know they're not going to want to hear about how

> many baptisms, or about how many—what kind of souls you've saved, it just doesn't make sense to them. They really want to know and understand if you're going to have an impact on homelessness, if you're going to help the social cohesion of the neighborhoods. What does it mean for you to care about the businesses that are located within two or three blocks of you and how are you going to support them? A real felt need for city members is what kind of parking impact is your church going to have?

But how is one to start? Again, Busby offers helpful advice on how to begin to cultivate a fruitful relationship with city officials:

> I think for church planters what I would highly recommend, finding out who your city council member is, wherever you want to plant, scheduling a meeting with them, just to ask questions. Do not tell them about your church. Ask them about what is going on in your district, what are the pain points, what are the things they're actually excited about in their district?

This is one of the areas where your city council member can help you a great deal. If you are new to a community, they can help orient you quickly to its specific needs and thus help you better understand how to serve and love it. The truth is, even if a church has been in a neighborhood for a while, in most cases their city council member is going to know the community far better than they do. This is primarily owing to the fact that in order to do their job well, a council member has to know all of the various constituencies in their district, not just one group.

Settlements Planting Settlements

One of the characteristics of early Irish abbots like Columbanus was that they planted monastic settlements that in turn planted other settlements. Eventually, the proliferation of these settlements resulted in networks of monasteries connected relationally that together had a greater influence on a region than single, isolated monasteries. Under Sorensen's leadership, Mission Chattanooga is pursuing a similar approach. Since its inception fourteen years ago, Mission Chattanooga has birthed three other missions: Mission Red Bank, Mission Cincinnati, and Mission Cleveland. While not identical to Mission Chattanooga, they share many of its same values and like MC are inspired by a passion to bring shalom to their respective communities. In recognition of Sorensen's work in Chattanooga and his help to planting other missions, Archbishop Foley Beach ordained him an abbot in the Anglican Church of North America.

The Black Church and Other Faith Traditions

In this work I've been looking at the early Irish monastics for insight on how the church can build Ben Op communities, namely: expand its sense of calling while using the built environment to more effectively advance the kingdom of God. We could just as easily and fruitfully look at the Black church for how to do this. In large part due to its marginalization and exclusion from broader societal institutions, the Black church has by necessity had to create its own institutions and had a more holistic cultural role. It has, by the same token, to a greater degree resisted the cultural marginalization of the White church. Therefore, this work is not written primarily for Black church leaders; by and large they're already familiar with many of the principles and themes laid out in this work. In fact, White pastors would do well to cultivate relationships with local Black urban pastors and learn from them.

Building the Benedict Option

In addition, if, as seems likely, our culture continues to become more hostile to Christianity, and faith in general, we may find that we have more in common with other faith communities than we have realized. Whether or not this is the case, there may be lessons to be learned from the way other faith communities are seeking to build and strengthen their respective communities in an increasingly hostile culture.

For example, there may be lessons we can learn from the way that the Hasidic Jewish community in New York City has maintained its cultural identity. You could argue that with the Hasidic town Kiryas Joel, founded in upstate New York, they've taken the principles argued for in this work much further than any contemporary Christian community has to date.[5]

There are encouraging signs, however, that Christians not just in America but abroad are beginning to relearn many of the truths known by the early Irish and look for ways to create communities that, broadly speaking, might be characterized as Ben Op

5. See, for instance, Myers and Stolzenberg, *American Shtetl*.

communities. While some of these are still only in the beginning stages, it will be interesting to see how they develop over time. Abbaye de la Lucerne is one such Catholic example in France (https://www.abbaye-lucerne.fr). Cascina San Benedetto is another Catholic community in Northern Italy. In the United States, Catholic communities have sprung up in Hyattsville, Maryland; Steubenville, Ohio; and Irving, Texas. Reformed Protestant communities include Moscow, Idaho, and a proposed village in Kentucky just north of Nashville, Tennessee, while Canton Abbey is a Celtic-inspired Anglican ministry in Canton, Ohio (https://cantonabbey.org). There are also similar movements developing among more progressive Christians. The Lindisfarne Community is one such (http://www.icmi.org).

While these communities may differ from one another in many respects, they do seem to share in common a conviction that new strategies and a commitment to authentic community are needed to sustain a genuine faith in an increasingly hostile culture. It will be interesting to see the degree to which such thinking continues to spread in the years ahead.

Chapter 13

Third Spaces and Starting a Ben Op Community from Scratch

Anyone caught up in the bad work of real estate development or architecture and building must consider how diligently the atheist has worked, how imaginatively he has constructed housing projects and public buildings to foster his religion; whereas Christians have behind them the best and loveliest housing developments in history in the Catholic villages of Europe, and fail to reproduce them. We visit them, take pictures of them, never dreaming we could live in them, when as a matter of fact it is feasible if not profitable to construct something like them even in the suburbs of New York or San Francisco, advertising them as Christian Heights or Flats! After all isn't that what names like Los Angeles and San Francisco once signified?

—John Senior,
The Restoration of Christian Culture

Church planters often look for a venue in which to meet and then launch public Sunday services hoping to attract a crowd. They build expectation through Facebook posts and live social media countdowns to launch date, all the while blanketing the area with a blizzard of direct mail invitations. When Chris Sorensen and his church planting team arrived in Chattanooga to plant their church, they utilized a different approach. Rather than immediately starting a Sunday service they made the creation of a third space central to their church planting strategy. Today many of our neighborhoods consist of an undifferentiated, homogenous sprawl of single-family homes lacking any social infrastructure around which community can gather. Therefore, Sorensen reasoned that creating a third space offered promise as a church planting strategy. In the case of Mission Chattanooga, because the team members all happened to be musicians, they decided to create a venue for live music. This strategy of planting a church by first creating a third space is increasingly being followed by a new generation of church planters, and should be considered by anyone seeking to create a Ben Op community.

One such church planter is Scott Pontier of Jamestown Harbor Church in Hudsonville, Michigan. Like Sorensen he drew inspiration from the example of the early Irish monastics and, again like Sorensen, he's been building his church planting strategy around the construction of a third space. As he puts it:

> In Ireland they [evangelized] by being a different kind of witness by moving into that community and building these monasteries, [monasteries] . . . designed to say, "You are now entering a different way of living." And the first building you came to was the guest house, not their church, not their guard shack, and the guest house was well appointed, they spent a lot of time making it inviting and it was for you, you could come and stay just inside the wall in this middling space between the world and the God centered community and learn and experience a new way of life. That's how I think about our church. Can our church be a guest house for our community? What does it mean to create space for people to come and experience a different way of life? And so if we can build a facility that does the

same thing, that's where the facility thinking really kind of captures it.[1]

This strategy was particularly useful for their suburban context. Pontier explains:

> One of the things that's true about a suburban context is that we're just adding houses. We're not planning around city centers. So our community is a community that doesn't have a center. Just the roads, the neighborhoods and some schools. So we've just thought a lot about, "What would it mean to be the center of our community? How do you put the gospel, the Good News, at the center of the community, if not literally, but figuratively?"

Jamestown Harbor Church (photo courtesy of Kristine Byrnes).

One way, Pontier reasoned, was to create a third space around which their community could begin to gather. But what type of third space? As they got to know their community, Pontier's group discovered that their community gathered around relationships and sports. Or as Pontier puts it, "Everybody's kids are in sports." So they decided to partner with a sports company called Michigan

1. Jacobsen and Proppe, "Social Infrastructure and the Church."

Third Spaces and Starting a Ben Op Community

Sports Academies with an eye ultimately, by building in stages, to create a sports complex. While the plan is still developing, it represents the type of "out of the box thinking" and use of third spaces that will become increasingly necessary in the years ahead if the church is to thrive.

Belonging Then Believing

In choosing to make a third space central to their church planting strategy, Sorensen and Pontier recognized an aspect of conversion often overlooked: "Belonging comes before believing."[2] Or, as sociologist Rodney Stark puts it, "Conversion isn't about seeking or embracing an ideology; it is about bringing one's religious behavior into alignment with that of one's friends and family members."[3] What this means is that people are often attracted to the love of a particular community, begin to participate in the life of that community, and then, over time bring their beliefs into alignment with those of the community itself. Crucial to such an approach is the community being open and welcoming to outsiders.

As George Hunter points out, this was the same approach to evangelism pursued by the Irish monastics:

1. They established community with people.
2. Within that community, they engaged in conversation, ministry, prayer, and worship with them.
3. In time, as the people discovered that they now believed, the monastics invited them to commit fully to a life of discipleship.[4]

With this in mind, if you're considering creating a Ben Op community from scratch, spend time praying about what needs your community has. Then consider creating a third space that could both serve that need and double as a meeting place for your nascent Ben Op on Sunday. Such a third space thus becomes a

---

2. Hunter, *Celtic Way of Evangelism*, 44 (quoting John Finney).
3. Stark, *Rise of Christianity*, 17.
4. Stark, *Rise of Christianity*, 43.

venue through which to build community, contribute to the overall health of your neighborhood, and meet people who might potentially join your budding faith community.

It is here that caution is in order, however. My wife and I served a church for nine years in Ithaca, New York. Some years before we came to town, another church purchased a beautiful, historic downtown building, and after investing a lot of sweat equity, returned it to its original glory. With gorgeous hardwood beams, a rich mellow interior, and an ornate pressed tin ceiling, it made for an amazing café and third space. Unfortunately, we quickly learned, as the rest of the community had, to avoid it. Why? Because one learned after visiting only a few times that, invariably, upon taking their seat they'd be approached within a matter of minutes by a well-meaning but somewhat pushy member of the church seeking to engage them in a spiritual conversation (whether the customer wanted one or not!). As a result, the café was not nearly as popular as it should have been. The community came to see that it was a third space created primarily to meet the church's need for gaining new members, rather than providing a tangible benefit to the community itself.

Chapter 14

The Importance of Navigators

All buildings, large or small, public or private, have a public face, a facade; they therefore, without exception, have a positive or negative effect on the quality of the public realm, enriching or impoverishing it in a lasting and radical manner. The architecture of the city and public space is a matter of common concern to the same degree as laws and language. They are the foundation of civility and civilization.
—Léon Krier, The Architecture of Community

So Much To Learn, So Little Time

Well-known business management guru Peter Drucker claimed that the two most difficult jobs are that of hospital administrator and pastor. Leading a church is extremely difficult on multiple levels and requires a pastor to be conversant in a number of disciplines. Therefore, if you are a church leader reading this and have gotten this far, right about now you're apt to feel a bit overwhelmed with all this talk of zoning, charrettes, and financing. Such things are typically not part of the skill set of church leaders. As Ryan Terry points out, one of the greatest hurdles to people getting into local development is simply not knowing "the basic stuff": "how to call an architect and enter a contract for services, how to deal with a contractor, how to call up a bank and ask for a loan."[1]

This is why if you're contemplating a construction project (particularly a Ben Op) it is absolutely essential to develop a relationship with a local Christian developer: someone who shares your values and whom you can trust, someone who can help you and your church navigate the complex world of urban planning and construction. Even the Irish themselves didn't come up with the idea of their monasteries *ex nihilo*. Very likely they were shown the way (or at least influenced) by monastic forerunners such as Martin of Tours in France, or those monks who fled into the arid wastes of the Egyptian desert.

But how to find such a developer? A great place to start is the Congress for the New Urbanism (CNU). They have local charters throughout the country, and so the first step would be to see if there's one in your area.

Congress for the New Urbanism (CNU) (https://www.cnu.org):

---

1. Congress for the New Urbanism, "Incremental Development."

The Importance of Navigators

> CNU works to empower people who want more great places built. [Their] wide array of programs, events, tools, and resources—from CNU membership to advocacy materials—are designed to accelerate the pace of change. With more than 2,600 members working in communities across North America, in urban centers and in historic small towns, CNU connects and empowers the professionals, leaders, advocates, and citizens creating places people love.[2]

The good news is that there are quite a few other organizations and resources that can help you navigate the world of urban development and chart your course forward.

Without a doubt, one of the most exciting of these groups is *Redemptification*. John Marsh, Ty Maloney, and the practitioners they interview will help you catch a vision for how the church can minister to its community through the built environment. They speak from years of hard-won experience and have a passion for "redemptification": the creative work of renewing a person or place to its intended beauty and glory" (http://redemptification.com).

Another place to go for inspiring stories and informative conversations revolving around placemaking is *The Embedded Church Podcast*. The podcast hosts, Eric O. Jacobsen and Sara Joy Proppe, interview faith-based practitioners who are ministering to their communities in a variety of ways, through the built environment (https://www.embeddedchurch.com).

On his YouTube channel *Not Just Bikes*, Jason Slaughter tells "stories of great urban planning and urban experiences from the Netherlands and beyond. There are a lot of reasons why Dutch cities are so great; it's not just bikes ..." (https://www.youtube.com/@NotJustBikes/featured).

One organization that can help equip you with the know-how to become a small developer is the aforementioned *Incremental Development Alliance (Inc Dev Alliance)*.

> The Incremental Development Alliance began in 2015 as a collaboration between small developers who found

---

2. Congress for the New Urbanism, "What Is New Urbanism?"

themselves overwhelmed by the number of people asking them the same question: how do I build a small building in the place I love? In order to share their mentorship and hard-won knowledge far and wide, the Alliance was created to structure a suite of classroom-based and hands-on coaching tools that could be scaled across the country for the benefit of municipal clients and developers alike.[3]

Inc Dev holds regular day-long intensive "Workshops" and "Bootcamps" to give those wanting to become small developers the skills they need to make their vision a reality.

The Strong Towns movement is another organization (and podcast) that will help you understand the dysfunction of our current way of planning cities and communities, as well as give you the knowledge and tools to help fix the problem.

> Strong Towns is a 501(c)(3) nonprofit media advocacy organization. We produce content that analyzes the failures of the post-war North American development pattern while giving citizens the knowledge and tools to start making our places better today. We seek to replace America's post-war pattern of development, the Suburban Experiment, with a pattern of development that is financially strong and resilient. We advocate for cities of all sizes to be safe, livable, and inviting. We work to elevate local government to be the highest level of collaboration for people working together in a place, not merely the lowest level in a hierarchy of governments.[4]

Another great resource is the *Proximity Project*, Sara Proppe's consulting company. Through it:

> She desires to equip churches to be strategic stewards of their properties for the common good within the contexts of their neighborhoods. Through the avenues of placemaking and real estate development, she empowers churches to

---

3. Inc Dev Alliance, "How We Got Started," §1.
4. Strong Towns, "About Us."

The Importance of Navigators

connect their mission and their story to their physical place in the neighborhood in creative and dynamic ways.[5]

I have found Sara incredibly responsive, and quick to (graciously) answer my many questions (https://www.proximityprojectinc.com).

If you are considering starting your own Ben Op community, I would love to serve as a resource and get you connected with others who are like-minded and who may help you in the pursuit of your goal. In addition, if you are looking to join a Ben Op community and are in the greater DC area, or might be willing to relocate, let's talk. I can be reached at: edwarddavis68@gmail.com

---

5. Jacobsen and Proppe, "Podcast Hosts."

Conclusion

The only really effective apologia for Christianity comes down to two arguments, namely the saints the church has produced and the art which has grown in her womb. Better witness is borne to the Lord by the splendour of holiness and art which have arisen in the community of believers than by clever excuses which apologetics has come up with to justify the dark sides which, sadly, are so frequent in the church's human history. If the church is to continue to transform and humanise the world, how can she dispense with beauty in her liturgies, that beauty which is so closely linked with love and with the radiance of the Resurrection? No. Christians must not be too easily satisfied. They must make their church into a place where beauty—and hence truth—is at home. Without this the world will become the first circle of hell.

—Pope Benedict XVI

In his work, *The Great Divorce*, C. S. Lewis paints an allegory in which a man takes a bus ride from hell to heaven. After wandering for hours in a drizzling rain through the dreary streets of a town comprised of "dingy lodging houses, small tobacconists, hoardings from which posters hung in rags, and windowless warehouses," the narrator find himself "in a busy queue by the side of a long, mean street," waiting to board a bus bound for he knows not where. After boarding, he eventually finds himself seated next to an intelligent looking man in a bowler hat:

> "It seems the deuce of a town," I volunteered, "and that's what I can't understand. The parts of it that I saw were empty. Was there once a much larger population?"
>
> "Not at all," said my neighbor. "The trouble is that they're so quarrelsome. As soon as anyone arrives he settles in some street.... Before the week is over, he's quarreled so badly that he decides to move... He'll move right out to the edge of town and build a new house.... That's how the town keeps on growing."
>
> "And what about the earlier arrivals? I mean—there must be people who came from earth to your town even longer ago."
>
> "That's right. There are. They've been moving on and on. Getting further apart.... Astronomical distances..."
>
> "Then the town will go on spreading indefinitely?" I said.
>
> "That's right."
>
> "Two fully inhabited streets would accommodate the people that are now spread over a million square miles of empty streets."[1]

The picture Lewis paints here is of a hell characterized by increasing atomization, fractured community, and a dreary urban landscape devoid of beauty. Nothing could better describe the reality of the modern American landscape as we have designed it over the past seventy years.

---

1. Lewis, *Great Divorce*, 471–73.

An altogether different picture of planned community is that of the New Jerusalem found in the book of Revelation.

> Then I saw a new heaven and a new earth, for the first heaven and the first earth had passed away, and the sea was no more. And I saw the holy city, new Jerusalem, coming down out of heaven from God, prepared as a bride adorned for her husband . . . And I saw no temple in the city, for its temple is the Lord God the Almighty and the Lamb. And the city has no need of sun or moon to shine on it, for the glory of God gives it light, and its lamp is the Lamb. By its light will the nations walk, and the kings of the earth will bring their glory into it, and its gates will never be shut by day—and there will be no night there. They will bring into it the glory and the honor of the nations. (Rev 21: 1–2, 22–26)

> Then the angel showed me the river of the water of life, bright as crystal, flowing from the throne of God and of the Lamb through the middle of the street of the city; also, on either side of the river, the tree of life with its twelve kinds of fruit, yielding its fruit each month. The leaves of the tree were for the healing of the nations. No longer will

CONCLUSION

there be anything accursed, but the throne of God and of the Lamb will be in it, and his servants will worship him. (Rev 22:1–3)

Rather than increasingly atomized individuals living each in their own private mansion separated by vast lawns, the image of the new created order is that of God's redeemed people living in a city clearly demarcated by walls and clothed in a beauty that takes one's breath away.

It is a city that by its very cube-like shape, the same as that of the Holy of Holies in Solomon's temple, signifies that it is the locus of God's presence. Because it is the locus of God's presence, it becomes the focal point of the nations of the earth. It is a vivid reminder to us that, in the words of Alexander Schmemann:

> *All that exists is God's gift to man, and it all exists to make God known to man, to make man's life communion with God ... God blesses everything He creates, and this means that He makes all creation the sign and means of His presence and wisdom, love and revelation: "O Taste and See that the Lord is Good!"*[2]

In short, matter ... matters. And therefore, as we look to create Benedict Option communities, steel God's people for the years ahead, and prepare the church to effectively minister to a post-Christian world, it behooves us to consider approaches that appreciate the importance of the built environment. By doing so, we can ensure that the buildings we construct will not sit empty during the week in a sea of asphalt, but rather serve as the nuclei for Ben Op communities: communities that will nurture the body of Christ and strengthen it to successively reach a post-Christian culture, while helping to counteract sprawl, repair our fraying social fabric, and create islands of community in the vast suburban wasteland so many of us live in. The Irish have shown the way. Do we have the courage and faith to follow?

---

2. Schmemann, *For the Life of the World*, 21.

Building the Benedict Option

Bibliography

Abrams, Samuel J. "What Are the Real Third Places?" *National Review*, Dec 12, 2021. https://www.nationalreview.com/2021/12/what-are-the-real-third-places/.

Alexander, Christopher, et al. *A Pattern Language: Towns, Building, Construction*. Oxford: Oxford University Press, 2018.

American Veterinary Medical Association. "2022 AVMA Pet Ownership and Demographics Sourcebook." Veterinary Economics Division, May 2022.

Anonymous. "Victor Papanek Post." *WrathofGnon* (blog), April 12, 2022. https://wrathofgnon.tumblr.com.

Barna Group. "Year in Review: Barna's Top 10 Releases of 2020." Dec 28, 2020. https://www.barna.com/research/year-in-review-2020/.

Bartrina, J. Aranceta. "Prevalence of Obesity in Developed Countries: Current Status and Perspectives." *Nutrición Hospitalria* (Feb 17, 2002) 31–41. https://pubmed.ncbi.nlm.nih.gov/11928534/.

Barzun, Jacques. *From Dawn to Decadence: 1500 to the Present*. New York: Harper Perennial, 2001.

Bauman, Zygmunt. *Liquid Modernity*. Cambridge, UK: Polity, 2000.

Bede. *History of the English Church and People*. Translated and introduction by Leo Sherley Price. New York: Dorset, 1955.

Bess, Philip. *Till We Have Built Jerusalem: Architecture, Urbanism and the Sacred*. Wilmington, DE: Intercollegiate Studies Institute, 2006.

Bitel, Lisa M. "Ekphrasis at Kildare: The Imaginative Architecture of a Seventh-Century Hagiographer." *Speculum* 79.3 (Jul 2004) 605–27. https://www.jstor.org/stable/20462975.

Blaff, Ari. "Six Figure Income Now Required to Afford Median Home." National Review, Nov 23, 2022. https://www.nationalreview.com/news/homeownership-now-an-exclusive-club-as-americans-earning-under-100k-struggle-to-stay-afloat-with-inflation/.

Blair, John. *The Church in Anglo-Saxon Society*. Oxford: Oxford University Press, 2005.

Bibliography

Bleich, Sara N., et al. "Why Is the Developed World Obese?" *Annual Review of Public Health* 29 (April 2008) 273–95. https://pubmed.ncbi.nlm.nih.gov/18173389/.

Boot, Max. "Americans' Ignorance of History Is a National Scandal." *Washington Post*, Feb 20, 2019. https://www.washingtonpost.com/opinions/americans-ignorance-of-history-is-a-national-scandal/2019/02/20/b8be683c-352d-11e9-854a-7a14d7fec96a_story.html.

Bowden, Johnny, and Stephen Sinatra. *The Great Cholesterol Myth*. Dover, DE: Fair Winds, 2020.

Cahill, Thomas. *How the Irish Saved Civilization: The Untold Story of Ireland's Heroic Role from the Fall of Rome to the Rise of Medieval Europe*. The Hinges of History 1. New York: Anchor, 1996.

Carragáin, Tomás Ó. "The Architectural Setting of the Mass in Early-Medieval Ireland." *Medieval Archaeology* 53 (2009) 119–54.

Centers for Disease Control and Prevention. "Overweight and Obesity: Adult Obesity Facts." Last updated May 17, 2022. https://www.cdc.gov/obesity/data/adult.html.

———. "Suicide Rising across the U.S." *CDC Vital Signs*, June 2018. https://www.cdc.gov/vitalsigns/pdf/vs-0618-suicide-H.pdf.

Chapin, Ross. *Pocket Neighborhoods*. Newtown, CT: Taunton, 2011.

Charen, Mona. "The Kids Are Not All Right." *Real Clear Politics*, June 2, 2017. https://www.realclearpolitics.com/articles/2017/06/02/the_kids_are_not_all_right_134078.html.

Charles-Edwards, T. M. *Early Christian Ireland*. Cambridge: Cambridge University Press, 2000.

Congress for the New Urbanism. "Incremental Development: A Movement." *On the Park Bench: A Public Square Conversation* (webinar), Mar 15, 2022. https://www.youtube.com/watch?v=dI28OfSBTYg&t=388s.

———. "What Is New Urbanism?" https://www.cnu.org/resources/what-new-urbanism.

Coulton, G. G. *Social Life in Britain from the Conquest to the Reformation*. London: Routledge, 2013.

Crams, Ralph Adams. *Walled Towns*. Australia: Leopold Classic Library, 2015.

Danube Institute. "An Evening with Rod Dreher—A Conversation with the Author of *Live Not By Lies*." YouTube video, Apr 19, 2022. https://www.youtube.com/watch?v=kG1tEZjRvLk&t=736s.

Delbridge, Emily. "What Is the True Cost of Owning a Car?" *The Balance*, Oct 25, 2021. https://www.thebalancemoney.com/true-car-ownership-costs-4165784.

Devlin, Bradley. "BlackRock Plots to Buy Ukraine." *American Conservative*, Dec 30, 2022. https://www.theamericanconservative.com/blackrock-plots-to-buy-ukraine/.

Dickinson, Greg. *Suburban Dreams*. Tuscaloosa: University of Alabama Press, 2015.

BIBLIOGRAPHY

Doherty, Charles. "The Monastic Town in Early Medieval Ireland." In *The Comparative History of Urban Origins in Non-Roman Europe: Ireland, Wales, Denmark, Germany, Poland and Russia from the Ninth to the Thirteenth Century*, edited by H. B. Clarke and Anngret Simms. Oxford, 1985.

Edwards, Nancy. *A New History of Ireland*. Vol. 1, *Prehistoric and Early Ireland*. Edited by Dáibhí Ó Cróinín. Oxford: Oxford University Press, 2005.

Esolen, Anthony. *Out of the Ashes: Rebuilding American Culture*. Washington, DC: Regnery, 2017.

Finney, John. *Recovering the Past: Celtic and Roman Missions*. London: Darton, Longman and Todd, 2011.

Fletcher, Richard. *The Barbarian Conversion*. New York: Henry Holt, 1998.

Forster, Walter O. *Zion on the Mississippi: The Settlement of the Saxon Lutherans in Missouri, 1839–1841*. St. Louis: Concordia, 1990.

Francis, Richard. *Fruitlands: The Alcott Family and Their Search for Utopia*. New Haven, CT: Yale University Press, 2010.

The German National Tourist Board. "Würzburg: World Heritage and Franconian Wine." https://www.germany.travel/en/cities-culture/wuerzburg.html.

Gladwell, Malcolm. *Outliers: Secret of Success*. New York: Little, Brown, 2008.

Gunaratna, Shanika. "Daily Step Counts: Which Countries Are Most Active—and Which Are Least?" *CBS News*, Jul 13, 2017. https://www.cbsnews.com/news/which-countries-most-walking-least-walking/.

Harvard Medical School. "National Comorbidity Survey (NCS)." August 21, 2017. https://www.hcp.med.harvard.edu/ncs/index.php.

Heid, Jim. "Lean Financing: Alternatives to Institutional Capital." *The Project for Lean Urbanism*. https://leanurbanism.org/wp-content/uploads/2016/12/Heid_Alternatives.pdf.

Henderson, Roger. "Kuyper's Inch." *Pro Rege* 36.3 (2008) 12–14.

Holmes, Baxter. "'These Kids Are Ticking Time Bombs': The Threat of Youth Basketball." *ESPN*, Jul 11, 2019. https://www.espn.com/nba/story/_/id/27125793/these-kids-ticking-bombs-threat-youth-basketball.

Honderich, Holly. "Panel Says U.S. Adults Should Get Routine Screening for Anxiety." *BBC News*, Sep 20, 2022. https://www.bbc.com/news/world-us-canada-62974686.

Hopkins, Gerard Manley. *Letters to Robert Bridges and Correspondence with Richard Watson Dixon*. Oxford: Oxford University Press, 1955.

Hunter, George G., III. *The Celtic Way of Evangelism*. Rev. ed. Nashville: Abingdon, 2010.

Hunter, James Davison. *To Change the World*. Oxford: Oxford University Press, 2010.

Inc Dev Alliance. "How We Got Started." https://www.incrementaldevelopment.org/alliance.

Jacobsen, Eric O., and Sara Joy Proppe. "Podcast Hosts." The Embedded Church. https://www.embeddedchurch.com/hosts.

BIBLIOGRAPHY

———. "Social Infrastructure and the Church." *The Embedded Church Podcast*, season 5, episode 2, July 12, 2022. https://the-embedded-church-podcast.simplecast.com/episodes/social-infrastructure.

———. "Third Place and the Church." *The Embedded Church Podcast*, season 5, episode 3, August 9, 2022. https://the-embedded-church-podcast.simplecast.com/episodes/third-place-and-the-church.

Johnson, Cat. "10 Tips for Designing Your Coworking Space or Shared Space." Satellite Deskworks Workspace Management Software, May 10, 2018.

Klinenberg, Eric. *Palaces for the People*. Danvers, MA: Crown, 2018.

Kosloski, Philip. "New Study: Beautiful Churches and Cathedrals an Important Force in Bringing Conversions." *Aleteia*, June 20, 2017. https://aleteia.org/2017/06/20/new-study-beautiful-churches-and-cathedrals-an-important-force-in-bringing-conversions/.

Kunstler, James Howard. *Home from Nowhere*. New York: Touchstone, 1998.

Lewis, C. S. *The Great Divorce*. Rev. ed. New York: HarperOne, 2009.

———. *A Mind Awake: An Anthology of C. S. Lewis*. Boston: Houghton Mifflin Harcourt, 2003.

Makridis, Christos A.. "Social Capital and Covid." *City Journal*, Dec 3, 2021. https://www.city-journal.org/article/social-capital-and-covid.

Marohn, Charles L. *Strong Towns: A Bottom-Up Revolution to Rebuild American Prosperity*. Hoboken, NJ: Wiley, 2019.

Marshall, Joey, et al. "Those Who Switched to Telework Have Higher Income, Education and Better Health." United States Census Bureau, Mar 31, 2021. https://www.census.gov/library/stories/2021/03/working-from-home-during-the-pandemic.html.

Marsh, John. "Incrementalism—Real Estate as Rainforest or Row Crops with Special Guest Aaron Lubeck." *Redemptification Podcast*. http://redemptification.com/?p=1633.

McClay, Wilfred M. "History as a Way of Knowing." *Law and Liberty*, Sep 17, 2021. https://lawliberty.org/history-as-a-way-of-knowing/.

McDonald, Danny. "'I'm at My Wit's End': Welcome to the Underbelly of the Region's Housing Crisis." *Boston Globe*, Nov 12, 2022. https://www.bostonglobe.com/2022/11/12/metro/im-my-wits-end-welcome-underbelly-regions-housing-crisis/.

Michaud, Marilyn. "A Turn to the Past: Republicanism and Brook Farm." In *The Literary Utopias of Cultural Communities, 1790–1910*, edited by Marguérite Corporaal and Evert Jan van Leeuwen, 67–81. New Haven, CT: Yale University Press, 2010.

Myers, David N., and Nomi M. Stolzenberg. *American Shtetl: The Making of Kiryas Joel, a Hasidic Village in Upstate New York*. Princeton, NJ: Princeton University Press, 2021.

National Community Church. "Ebenezer's Coffee House." https://national.cc/expressions/ebenezers-coffeehouse

BIBLIOGRAPHY

The National Community Survey. "Loudoun County, VA: Community Livability Report 2020." https://www.loudoun.gov/DocumentCenter/View/166655/Loudoun-County-Survey-of-Residents-2020.

National Park Service. "Utopias in America." https://www.nps.gov/articles/utopias-in-america.htm.

Niermann, Matthew. "Comfort or Beauty? Assessing Aesthetics and Mission in Protestant Church Design." *The Institute for Sacred Architecture* 35 (Spring 2019). https://www.sacredarchitecture.org/articles/comfort_or_beauty_assessing_aesthetics_and_mission_in_protestant_church_des.

Nixon, Jude V., and Noel Barber, eds. *The Collected Works of Gerard Manley Hopkins*. Vol. 5, *Sermons and Spiritual Writings*. Oxford: Oxford University Press, 2019.

Nooga Today Intern. "Visit Chattanooga's MLK District." *Nooga Today*, Jan 15, 2021. https://noogatoday.6amcity.com/visit-chattanoogas-mlk-district.

Parolek, Daniel. "Missing Middle Housing: Thinking Big and Building Small to Respond to Today." *Strong Towns* (webcast), Aug 11, 2020. https://www.youtube.com/watch?v=oSIBvDgUUKQ&t=4s.

———. "Q and A: Missing Middle." *Strong Towns* (webcast), Aug 13, 2020. https://www.youtube.com/watch?v=VfJUP1YvkKk.

Patrick. "The Confession of St. Patrick." Eternal Word Television Network, 1996. https://www.ewtn.com/catholicism/library/confession-of-st-patrick-5728.

Pavlac Glyer, Diana. *The Company They Keep: C. S. Lewis and J. R. R. Tolkien as Writers in Community*. Kent, OH: Kent State University Press, 2007.

Pew Research Center. "Modeling the Future of Religion in America." Sep 13, 2022. https://www.pewresearch.org/religion/2022/09/13/modeling-the-future-of-religion-in-america/.

Postman, Neil. *Amusing Ourselves to Death: Public Discourse in the Age of Show Business*. New York: Penguin, 2005.

Proppe, Sara Joy, and Edward Dunar. *Redemptive Placemaking: A Toolkit for Discerning Your Church's Mission in the Built Environment*. Proximity Project. https://www.proximityprojectinc.com/placemaking-toolkit.

Proximity Project. "About." https://www.proximityprojectinc.com/about.

Putnam, Robert. "Bowling Alone: America's Declining Social Capital. An Interview with Robert Putnam." *Journal of Democracy* 6.1 (Jan 1995) 65–78.

Ratcliffe, Janneke. "How We Can Solve the Nation's Affordable Housing Crisis." *CNN Business*, Feb 16, 2022. https://www.cnn.com/2022/02/16/perspectives/affordable-housing-crisis/index.html.

Renn, Aaron. "In Praise of the Private Good (Newsletter #66)." YouTube video, Jul 18, 2022. https://www.youtube.com/watch?v=3QJkCk4n4Ck&t=295s.

Requena Pelegri, Teresa. "Nathaniel Hawthorne's Minority Report on Transcendentalism." In *The Literary Utopias of Cultural Communities 1790–1910*, edited by Marguérite Corporaal and Evert Jan van Leeuwen, 93–112. New Haven, CT: Yale University Press, 2010.

BIBLIOGRAPHY

Roe, Jenny, and Layla McCay. "Author's Forum on Urbanism—Restorative Cities: Urban Design for Mental Health and Wellbeing." Congress for the New Urbanism, *On the Park Bench: A Public Square Conversation*, (webinar), Oct 12, 2021. https://www.cnu.org/resources/on-the-park-bench/authors-forum-urbanism--Restorative-Cities-urban-design-for-mental-health-and-wellbeing.

Rozenman, Eric. "Like David McCullough, Americans' Ignorance of History Should Keep Us up At Night." *Federalist*, Feb 4, 2020. https://thefederalist.com/2020/02/04/like-david-mccullough-americans-ignorance-of-history-should-keep-us-up-at-night/.

Sayers, Dorothy. "Why Work?" In *Letters to a Diminished Church: Passionate Arguments for the Relevance of Christian Doctrine*, 103–20. Nashville: Thomas Nelson, 2004.

Senior, John. *The Restoration of Christian Culture*. Norfolk, VA: IHS Press, 2008.

Sheldrake, Philip. *Living between Worlds: Place and Journey in Celtic Spirituality*. Boston: Cowley, 1996.

Schmemann, Alexander. *For the Life of the World: Sacraments and Orthodoxy*. Yonkers, NY: St. Vladimir's Seminary Press, 2018.

Smith, James K. A. *Desiring the Kingdom*. Grand Rapids: Baker Academic, 2013.

———. *How (Not) To Be Secular*. Grand Rapids: Eerdmans, 2014.

———. *You Are What You Love*. Grand Rapids: Brazos, 2016.

Soifer, Don. "Americans Are Dangerously Ignorant of History." Lexington Institute, Apr 12, 2011. https://www.lexingtoninstitute.org/americans-are-dangerously-ignorant-of-history/.

Stark, Rodney. *The Rise of Christianity*. Princeton, NJ: Princeton University Press, 1996.

Stone, Lyman. "Promise and Peril: The History of American Religiosity and Its Recent Decline." American Enterprise Institute, Apr 30, 2020. https://www.aei.org/research-products/report/promise-and-peril-the-history-of-american-religiosity-and-its-recent-decline/.

Streeter, Ryan. "Wanted: Better Neighborhoods." *City Journal*, Feb 6, 2020. https://www.city-journal.org/article/wanted-better-neighborhoods.

Strong Towns. "About Us." https://www.strongtowns.org/about.

Sullivan, Andrew. "The Poison We Pick." *New York Magazine*, Feb 19, 2018. https://nymag.com/intelligencer/2018/02/americas-opioid-epidemic.html.

Sussman, Ann, and Justin B. Hollander. *Cognitive Architecture: Designing For How We Respond to the Built Environment*. London: Routledge, 2021.

Swift, Catherine. "Forts and Fields: A Study of 'Monastic Towns' in Seventh and Eighth Century Ireland." *Journal of Irish Archeology* 9 (1998) 105–25.

Szymanski, Boleslaw, et al. "Social Consensus through the Influence of Committed Minorities." *Physical Review E* 84.1 (Jul 22, 2011).

Taylor, Charles. *A Secular Age*, Cambridge, MA: Belknap, 2007.

Tripkovic, Jovan. "Columnist Rod Dreher Talks Orthodoxy and Nationalism Religion." *Religion Unplugged*, Oct 28, 2022. https://religionunplugged.

com/news/2022/10/28/qampa-rod-dreher-talks-orthodox-christianity-and-nationalism.

Twenge, Jean M. "Have Smart Phones Destroyed a Generation?" *Atlantic*, Sep 2017. https://www.theatlantic.com/magazine/archive/2017/09/has-the-smartphone-destroyed-a-generation/534198/.

Urban Land Institute. *What's Next? Real Estate in the New Economy*. Washington, DC: Urban Land Institute, 2011.

Wilken, Robert Louis. "The Church as Culture." *First Things*, April 2004. https://www.firstthings.com/article/2004/04/the-church-as-culture.

Zaleski, Philip, and Carol Zaleski. *The Fellowship: The Literary Lives of the Inklings*. New York: Farrar, Straus and Giroux, 2015.

Zippia. "Tennis Player Demographics and Statistics in the U.S." https://www.zippia.com/tennis-player-jobs/demographics/.

www.ingramcontent.com/pod-product-compliance
Lightning Source LLC
Chambersburg PA
CBHW070907160426
43193CB00011B/1392